Use Cases

Requirements
in Context

Second Edition

B. D. BARNRS

BAKER BARNRS ASSOC, INC.
9/04

Use
Cases

Requirements
in Context

Second Edition

DARYL KULAK AND EAMONN GUINEY
with illustrations by Erin Lavkulich

✦✦ Addison-Wesley

Boston • San Francisco • New York • Toronto • Montreal
London • Munich • Paris • Madrid
Capetown • Sydney • Tokyo • Singapore • Mexico City

The publisher offers discounts on this book when ordered in quantity for bulk purchases and special sales. For more information, please contact:

U.S. Corporate and Government Sales
(800) 382-3419
corpsales@pearsontechgroup.com

For sales outside of the U.S., please contact:

International Sales
(317) 581-3793
international@pearsontechgroup.com

Visit Addison-Wesley on the Web: www.awprofessional.com

Library of Congress Cataloging-in-Publication Data
Kulak, Daryl, 1963–
        Use cases: requirements in context / Daryl Kulak, Eamonn Guiney.—2nd ed.
            p. cm.
        Includes bibliographical references and index.
        ISBN 0-321-15498-3 (alk. paper)
        1. System design. 2. Use cases (Systems engineering) I. Guiney, Eamonn, 1971– II. Title.

QA76.9.S88K85 2003
658'.05421—dc21

                                                                        2003051832

ISBN 0-321-15498-3
Text printed on recycled paper
1 2 3 4 5 6 7 8 9 10—CRS—0706050403
First printing, July 2003

To Tamara, my wonderful wife
To my parents, Eunice and Wayne
To my brothers and sisters, Shelley, Todd, Keith, and Zena
D. K.

For Lara
E. G.

Contents

2 Moving to Use Cases   21

3 A Use-Case-Driven Approach to Requirements Gathering   53

8   Requirements Traceability   149

Preface

It has been an interesting three years since the first edition of this book was published. At that time, use cases were still an "interesting technique" but had not been widely adopted. Today, we see a software development marketplace where use cases are the standard practice for gathering requirements and have even migrated to other applications, including business processes and service offerings. We would not have predicted this wave of popularity in our happiest visions.

Of course, our book was not the only one in the last few years to proselytize use cases. But it has been gratifying to be part of this new technique's recognition in the software world. Given this trend, we've decided to publish a second edition of *Use Cases*, putting together the lessons we've learned since our original thoughts. And the lessons have been many. Our approach in the first edition was something we had created after several use-case-driven project efforts, but it was still a young process. Using it on many more projects since the book was published, we have had a chance to collaborate with many of the best minds in the software business and fine-tune the process into something much more workable, practical, and scaleable. We have also taken ideas from other emerging fields, including the ideas of **chaordic organizations** (Dee Hock 2000; Margaret Wheatley 2001; and others) as well as Drs. Theodore Williams and Hong Li of Purdue University and their **Purdue Enterprise Reference Architecture.** Both bodies of work have had a tremendous impact on how we've applied use cases on our projects and how we've recast our ideas in this new edition.

First and most noticeably, we have only three "F" iterations this time: Facade, Filled, and Focused. The last F (Finished) has proven troublesome on one project after another. First of all, in an iterative approach, nothing is ever truly *finished*. It is always evolving. Also, as an iteration, it really contained only the mesh between use cases and the user interface design. We have moved the user interface ideas into the Facade iteration because the evolution of the user interface should proceed in parallel with the creation of early use cases, not following it.

Another big change is our approach in our management chapter. Although we are not directly contradicting anything from before, we have expanded our explanation of iterative/incremental use-case-driven project management greatly in this edition. We call it holistic iterative/incremental, or HI/I (hi-eye). We believe this area of the lifecycle requires the most work of anything, since the waterfall project management processes from years past are not keeping up with the faster pace, more "chaordic" software lifecycles of today. We present our chapter on management here, but we eagerly look forward to other authors expanding on these ideas and inventing new ways of tackling this big problem. Also, the Project Management Institute (PMI) has made some gestures toward embracing some of the new software lifecycle ideas.

The appendixes in our first edition were regarded by many readers we heard from as the best and the worst parts of the book. We were the first to try to show partially complete use cases in our examples, which is a crucial step to understanding the iterative nature of use case creation. However, the presentation was quite confusing, because we repeated use cases through the four iterations, sometimes they changed, sometimes they didn't, and it was hard to tell what changed and when. This time we're taking a very different approach. We still want to tell the story of how use cases are applied to software requirements gathering, but we're doing it in a much less formal way. In each appendix, we've picked a style of application (large business application, technical subsystem, package evaluation, and so on) and shown how the use cases and other artifacts evolve through the story. We hope this will retain the good aspects of the first edition, but add some coherence to the evolution of use case versions.

We've found on many, many projects that the idea of use case hierarchies does nothing but add confusion. Creating use cases that are "high level" and then "detailed" use cases later is hurting the requirements process. Hierarchies that are taller and more complex (some books advocate four-level hierarchies or more) create more and more distance from the original business requirements. Even though our original process had only two levels of hierarchy (system context-level use case and one level below) we always had trouble with teams who wanted to add levels and confuse themselves. Similarly, using <<include>> and <<extend>> stereotypes on use case associations adds an unnecessary level of problems, which has caused us to eliminate their usage except in very specific circumstances. To this end, we've added a new tool to our familiar set of tools and filters: **the hierarchy killer.** We hope you have fun killing hierarchies everywhere.

Use cases are different from other types of requirements techniques in many ways, but one particular difference is in the realm of traceability. Use cases are much more traceable back to the business needs, and also traceable into the software development artifacts, to everything from UML analysis and design artifacts to testing, documentation, training, security, and even parts of the architecture. We've decided to dedicate a chapter to this traceability phenomenon of use cases, to show opportunities for making sure the team is "working on the right thing."

Finally, in the interests of keeping up-to-date with the technological tools of requirements gathering, we've listed the tools available at this writing and given some ideas as to their best use. Since these tools change so quickly (and books get written so slowly, especially by us!) we decided to keep this brief.

We hope you enjoy this second edition of *Use Cases: Requirements in Context.* We've enjoyed creating the updates and going through the publishing cycle again with our publishers at Pearson Education. Please feel free to contact us with your ideas, experiences, and comments anytime. Our e-mail addresses are listed at the end of the last chapter in the book.

Acknowledgments

We would like to thank everyone who helped us with this second edition. We would especially like to thank Bill Banze, Jordan Antonelli, and Lara Hoekstra. Thanks also to the Addison-Wesley editorial and production teams: Peter Gordon, Bernard Gaffney, Lynda D'Arcangelo, and Tyrrell Albaugh.

Preface to the First Edition

Use Cases: Requirements in Context originally came about, as most books probably do, as the result of a complaint. We felt that there weren't any good books that addressed use cases for requirements gathering. It seemed that a lot of people agreed that use cases were a perfectly good tool to solve the requirements problem, but no one had put down on paper any detailed process to help people understand how to use them this way.

Requirements gathering has been a problem on almost every project we've been involved with. The fuzzy nature of requirements makes working with them slippery and unintuitive for most software analysts. Use cases are the first tool we've seen that addresses the specification and communication concerns usually associated with requirements gathering.

Although use cases in themselves are quite intuitive, the process around them is often done poorly. The questions that people have—How many iterations do I do? How fine-grained should a use case be?—are not answered or even addressed in most texts. This is probably because they are hard questions and the answers can vary greatly from one situation to another. However, they are important questions, and we decided to describe our own best practices as a first volley in what we hope will become a spirited industry dialog on how to generate requirements that will address user needs.

Use Cases: Requirements in Context is a practical book for the everyday practitioner. As consultants in the information technology industry, we employ use cases to specify business systems as part of our daily lives. We think we understand the issues facing people when they deliver software using tools such as the Unified Modeling Language and use cases. Our main intent is not to describe use case notation, although we do address that. Instead, we show a requirements process that addresses requirements gathering in a way that produces quality results.

While writing, we considered the factors that cause problems in requirements gathering, and we developed a use case method for delivering a requirements-oriented set of deliverables. The methodology breaks down the activity of producing requirements into a series of steps, and it answers the questions that usually come up when people employ use cases. This book relates directly to the real work of delivering a specification, managing that effort with a team, and getting the most bang for your buck.

We hope you enjoy this book. It was a labor of love for us. This is a process that works well for us. If it works for you, too, that's great. If it doesn't, perhaps you can adapt some of the tools, ideas, or suggestions to your own way of addressing the requirements problem.

Acknowledgments

Heartfelt thanks go to the numerous people who helped with this project. Some of them provided material aid and advice; all of them provided enthusiasm and encouragement throughout the project. It is an impossible task to mention everyone, but we would especially like to thank Bill Banze, Craig Larson, Steve Frison, Peter Gordon, Mat Henshall, Erin Lavkulich, John Lavkulich, Sam Starr, Terry Noreault, Jeanne Baker, Steve Ulrich, Ken Ricketts, Hong Li, Ted Williams, Lisa Austin, Naomi Kunkel, Jennifer Werth, Tracie Bennett, Vishal Saboo, Bill Klos, Karen Sander, Tamara Oakley, Debbie Ard, Paul Reed, Steve Jackson, Sarah Ward, and Ogden Weary.

1

When faced with what they
believe is a problem, most
engineers rush into offering
solutions.

—Alan M. Davis

The Trouble with Requirements

1.1 First and Least of All . . .

Technical people often pay much more attention to an entity relationship diagram or class diagram than to a requirements list.

Each time a team of systems people sets out to provide a computer system for a group of business people, they proceed through a set of activities that is fairly consistent:

- Requirements gathering
- Analysis
- Design
- Construction
- Testing
- Deployment
- Maintenance

The emphasis that the team gives each phase determines the direction and quality of the resulting computer system. If one activity is not given its due, there will be predictable problems with the project and the end product. In reality, however, certain activities usually receive more attention than do other activities. It is not easy to explain why this occurs, but it does. The activities that are usually ignored or paid lip service are

- Requirements gathering
- Testing
- Deployment
- Maintenance

Traditionally, fewer vendors brandish flashy tools to accomplish these activities, and maybe that's why they are less interesting and less appealing to practitioners. Certainly, a great deal of creativity and a wide range of skills are required by each activity, but the perception has been that anything other than the big three—analysis, design, and construction—does not require much attention or imagination.

This perception is slowly changing, in no small part because vendors are building tools to manage requirements (Rational RequisitePro, Borland Caliber RM, Telelogic DOORS), automate testing (Segue SilkTest/SilkPerformer, Mercury Interactive WinRunner/LoadRunner, Rational Robot/TeamTest/TestManager), and to facilitate rollout (Borland Deployment Server/Java, Marimba Desktop/Mobile, BEA WebLogic). Maintenance has also received a small boost with the need for Y2K remediation in recent years. We have opinions on ways to improve the visibility, appeal, and effectiveness of these other underappreciated activities, but we'll spare you those points until our next book.

We wrote this book because we care about requirements. In the first place, effective requirements are pivotal to producing a system that meets the needs of the users. It's no exaggeration to say that the requirements *themselves* are the needs of the users.

Moreover, we have grown to care about requirements because we have seen more projects stumble or fail as a result of poor requirements than for any other reason. Because requirements are meant to drive the rest of systems development, any small misstep is amplified into a major flaw by the time deployment is in progress. Correcting those flaws becomes extremely time-consuming (read: expensive!) because so much work has been put into heading in the wrong direction. Unfortunately, requirements do not translate neatly into one discrete module in a coded computer system. Sometimes, they are embodied in principles that cut across many code libraries and components. Because requirements are so abstract and so different from computer programs, it is difficult for people whose skills lie in the concrete aspects of computer programming to get them right.

Traditionally, requirements gathering

- Takes too long
- Documents the wrong thing
- Makes assumptions about activities that haven't happened yet
- Is often completed just in time to do it over again, thanks to swift and dramatic changes in the business

A short time ago, we came across a requirements definition document that contained more than 160 pages of "requirements." The sheer volume of this requirements list was enough to cause us to be filled with panic (or at least dread) at the thought of reading it and attempting to put the pieces together. Table 1.1 contains a sample of the requirements list (which is not very different from many other lists we've seen).

Table 1.1   Example of a Requirements List

Requirement	Definition
6.7.1.4.2	The system must provide the capability to capture all of the customer transactions for the fiscal year.
6.7.1.4.3	The system will provide restricted remote inquiry access (via dial-in) to view images and data separately or simultaneously.
6.7.1.4.4	The system will barcode documents automatically prior to distribution. At a minimum, the codes will be used to identify to which work queue the documents should be routed within the organization when they are returned.
6.7.1.4.5	When a workflow is initiated, the system must be able to prefetch the documents that are in electronic image format by document type or grouping of documents by process.
6.7.1.4.6	The system must create an entry in the journal file whenever a letter is created.
6.7.1.4.7	The system must maintain a list of current, open work processes and identify the work process to be executed and the workflow queue for the process. When particular documents are scanned, the system will determine whether there is a process open for that Social Security Number (SSN). If there is an open process, the system will route the document to the appropriate workflow queue, display the work process script, and highlight the current work process.

Don't forget this list continues for another 159 pages!

We dissect these and other requirements statements later, but you can imagine how difficult it would be to read large volumes of information at this level, much less to separate the true requirements from trivialities. If you are reading this book, you have probably lived this problem.

One reason that requirements documents are often so bad is that requirements gathering frequently follows an unproductive route. For example, it may be ignored; in that case, the development team jumps to a solution, resulting in a design based on unwritten and not agreed-upon assumptions about how the system should work. Or requirements gathering becomes an end in itself, and pages of "requirements" are gathered, documented, cross-referenced, and distributed, resulting in analysis paralysis and cancellation of the project before the rest of the lifecycle can even be started. Or the requirements may be dictated by a single user, system owner, or high-ranking manager, resulting in a system that works only for that person, to the dissatisfaction of everyone else. None of these methods produces satisfactory input to the analysis activity.

Hundreds of application lifecycle activities definitions, taken from various methodologies and processes, litter our bookshelves and the Internet. In Table 1.2 we provide our definitions of these terms because we build on these definitions to explain how to best approach requirements gathering.

Table 1.2   Activity Definitions

Activity Name	Description
Requirements gathering[a]	Gather and document the functions that the application should perform for the users in the users' language and from the users' perspective.
Analysis	Begin with the requirements and build a logical solution that satisfies the requirements but does not necessarily take the physical constraints into account.
Design	Begin with the logical solution and change it to work effectively with the physical constraints (network latency, database performance, user interface, caching, availability, and so forth) and produce specifications that can direct the construction effort.
Construction	Use the physical solution to produce working code, which involves making the lowest-level design decisions, writing code, compiling, debugging, and testing by increment.
Testing	Use the constructed application to produce a complete working system by system testing, detecting, and recording issues, fixing problems, and getting user acceptance of the result.

Activity Name	Description
Deployment	Fit the tested application into the production environment by deploying the code libraries to the destined machines, training the users, and fine-tuning the business procedures surrounding the new system.
Maintenance	Administer and make changes to the working system in the production environment to adapt to ongoing business changes (legislative, competitive), technology changes (hardware, software, and communications), physical changes (location, configuration), personnel (information technology [IT], user), system issues (code bugs, design problems) and even office politics.

a. We consider requirements gathering a separate activity from analysis. This is perhaps contrary to other prominent industry luminaries, who lump them together. Neither way is ultimately correct or incorrect; we have simply chosen to separate these activities to emphasize their importance.

Our definitions of lifecycle activities are not taken from any specific methodology. Instead, we've attempted to choose the most commonly used names and definitions for each term. Notice we've chosen the word *activity* instead of the word *phase*. We do this deliberately. In waterfall lifecycles, activities (or workflows), and phases are synonymous. However, *activity* relates to something that a person or group does. *Phase* implies specific start and stop times, dependencies, and a sequence. With iterative/incremental lifecycles, on the other hand, phases and activities are quite different. (We explain our approach to iterative/incremental lifecycles in Chapter 7.) Activities are done iteratively and incrementally, but phases are simply project management milestones that indicate a number of increments or a natural break in the lifecycle. For example, the Rational Unified Process (RUP) has the following workflows (activities): business modeling, requirements, analysis and design, implementation, test, deployment, configuration/change management, project management, and environment. It also has the following phases: inception, elaboration, construction, transition, and evolution. We see most methodologies moving in the same direction as the RUP to accommodate developers' as well as project managers' viewpoints.

1.2 What Is a Requirement?

Requirements are the effects that the computer is to exert in the problem domain, by virtue of the computer's programming.

—BENJAMIN L. KOVITZ

A *requirement* is something that a computer application must do for its users. It is a specific function, feature, quality, or principle that the system must provide in order for it to merit its existence. Requirements constitute part of the *scope* of a software development project. Add a few requirements, and the scope increases; take some away, and the scope decreases. The requirements also dictate how the system should respond to user interaction. It should do specific things when poked or prodded by the user in a certain way.

Requirements often seem abstract and intangible, especially to software developers. Requirements and design tend to blur together in a software person's brain until they become indistinguishable. However, it is crucial to keep requirements and design separate. Following are some of the ways IT people typically get off track with requirements:

- *Design considerations*—Anything that relates to *how* the system should operate, rather than *what* it needs to accomplish, is *design*. Design should not be part of requirements.
- *Vagueness*—If a requirement does not contribute positively to shaping the application design, it is too vague to be useful.
- *The use of computer industry language*—Requirements must always be phrased in the users' language. Jargon is OK as long as it's the users' jargon!
- *Relating to the business goals*—Every requirement must clearly relate to the goals of the businesspeople.

For clarification of this thorny issue, let's look again at the unfortunate requirements shown earlier in Table 1.1. This time let's look at them in detail and try to identify those things that do not constitute high-quality requirements.

> The system must provide the capability to capture all of the customer transactions for the fiscal year.

This requirement is too vague. How could it translate into a valuable constraint on the design of an application? It implies that the fiscal year has some impact on how customer transactions are organized, but we are not sure *what* impact. In fact, what is a "customer transaction"? We understand that this system has some type of data entry, but that must be stated more specifically. Maybe this is a suggestion about volume, meaning that old transactions can't be archived until they are a year old, but that interpretation is a stretch from looking at this requirement.

> The system will provide restricted remote inquiry access (via dial-in) to view images and data separately or simultaneously.

Saying "restricted" access is OK, but details about the restriction (who can, who can't) must be stated clearly in this context. Also vague is the reference to remote inquiry. How remote? Saying "remote access" when referring to mobile employees working in the field but still within a couple of miles of the office is one thing—but talking about worldwide access is yet another. Implications on the system design and architecture could be huge.

> The system will barcode documents automatically prior to distribution. At a minimum, the codes will be used to identify to which work queue the documents should be routed within the organization when they are returned.

This requirement makes several technical assumptions concerning the design. Barcoding is a solution to a problem, not a requirement. This system probably needs a way to identify each document uniquely, but it doesn't have to be barcodes. If all the existing systems use document barcoding (not the case with this system), it would make sense to write a nonfunctional requirement that states, "Unique identification of all documents will be done through barcoding." What's the difference? By embedding the barcoding assumption in various functional requirements, you make it difficult for someone to change the identification method from barcoding to glyphs, optical character recognition (OCR), or some other technology, thereby reducing your ability to respond to user needs discovered later in the process.

Another sticky point in this requirement is the reference to work queues. This seems to make an assumption about a workflow-oriented system. Workflow tools are solutions, not requirements. A better way to put it might have been, "At a minimum, the unique identification will ensure routing to a specific worker in the organization when the documents are returned."

> When a workflow is initiated, the system must be able to prefetch the documents that are in electronic image format by document type or grouping of documents by process.

Look at the reference to a *workflow*. Our suspicions were right! The requirements document has already specified a workflow solution in its requirements. Actually, this whole entry is suspicious. It seems to be saying that we must cache documents by two different criteria: by type or by process. The criteria are good requirements, but the caching (or prefetching) is really a solution to address performance problems and probably is not a requirement in itself.

> The system must create an entry in the journal file whenever a letter is created.

This requirement assumes the presence of a journal file, which has entries put into it when a letter is created. This requirement seems focused on the front end ("do this") instead of the back end ("in order to get this"). Why put entries into a journal file? You might do that so that you could create a list of all the letters that were created, when, and by whom. You really want the ability to audit letters written. Looking at it from the back end actually makes for a better, clearer requirement. You could create a journal file, but don't think about that until design!

The system must maintain a list of current, open work processes and identify the work process to be executed and the workflow queue for the process. When particular documents are scanned, the system will determine whether there is a process open for that SSN. If there is an open process, the system will route the document to the appropriate workflow queue, display the work process script, and highlight the current work process.

Again, this requirement seems more focused on the *how* than the *what*. Rather than look at the different steps a system must go through, it should clearly document the end in mind. Here is our rewrite for this requirement: "When a new document image is brought into the system, it should be routed to the worker who has the account open for the same SSN as the new document and should be made obvious to that worker. If no worker has an open account, the document should be made available to any worker."

You will also see that none of the requirements in our list are linked to a business person. It would be very difficult to pinpoint "who cares" about each of these requirements. Who are the computer users who will gain value from these requirements? The answers to these questions are not clear from these requirement statements.

But why not include design in requirements? Why do we keep harping on keeping design out of requirements?

There are several reasons. First, skill sets for a development project are matched to the activity performed. Therefore, the people who are gathering requirements probably have skills that are not suited to design or development. Furthermore, the designers/developers may not have the skills to conduct good quality user interviews and requirements planning sessions. It is also important to keep these activities separate because the design ultimately must be based on the requirements of the business.

Documenting requirements is an effort in understanding the problem at hand. Designing is the activity of solving the problem. The solution for the problem must come after the problem has been identified, documented, understood, and agreed on.

This can be tricky, especially in an iterative/incremental lifecycle. Perhaps a more accurate way to state our rule is that *no system, subsystem, or increment should proceed into design until the requirements for that system, subsystem, or increment have been identified, documented, and understood.* (Clumsy sentence structure, but good advice.) When design precedes requirements, or supplants them, the system takes on requirements of its own—requirements that are neither documented nor representative of the users' needs. The end result can be a wasted design effort, an unusable system, missed milestones, and unhappy users. Not knowing the problem that your design is solving is dangerous business. It is always advisable (if difficult) to define the problem completely before designing.

Another reason to keep design out of requirements gathering is related to the team environment. If a group is designing a system with no documented requirements, it is likely that group members will be working with different goals in mind. Because they do not have a common document from which to begin, they form the requirements picture in their own minds and use that to formulate their designs. These designs almost certainly will be incompatible and overlapping, causing integration problems, skipped requirements, scope creep, schedule issues, and unhappy users.

1.2.1 Functional Requirements

> *Without requirements, there is no way to validate a program design —*
> *that is, no way to logically connect the program to the*
> *customer's desires.*
>
> —Benjamin L. Kovitz

Functional requirements are what the users need for the system to work. Functional requirements are functions and features. These are the requirements we typically think of when we describe systems.

Here are some sample functional requirements for an order entry system:

- The system shall accept orders for products and provide notification to the entry clerk as to whether there is sufficient inventory to fulfill the order.
- The system shall use reorder points set by the inventory clerk to order new parts automatically.
- The system shall substitute comparable parts for parts that are out of stock as specified by the inventory manager.
- The system shall produce a nightly report of the orders for the previous day.

Use cases, the subject of this book, are one way to document functional requirements. We'll examine alternatives to use cases later in this chapter.

1.2.2 Nonfunctional Requirements

Nonfunctional requirements address the hidden areas of the system that are important to the users even though they may not realize it. As you can probably judge by the name, these requirements do not deal with the functionality of a system. Nonfunctional requirements are the global, fuzzy factors or principles that relate to the system's overall success. Many of them end in *-ility*, so we sometimes call the collection of them the *-ilities*. An example of an -ility is scalability: the ability of the system to handle an increased workload without significantly increasing the transaction processing time. (See Section 4.2.10 for details.)

1.3 Requirements Gathering, Definition, and Specification

Homeowner: "Hey, I wanted that foundation laid over there!"

Requirements gathering is the activity of bringing requirements together. *Requirements definition* is the activity of documenting these requirements and organizing them into something understandable and meaningful. A *requirements specification* is the document that results from the requirements activities.

As the first activity in the lifecycle of application development,[1] requirements gathering sets the stage for the rest of the work. A shoddy or incomplete requirements specification causes the analysis, design, and construction to be based on a shaky foundation—or worse, based on a foundation built in the wrong place entirely. An appropriate and complete requirements specification does nothing to ensure a successful implementation; however, *it makes it possible.*

---

1. Depending on the context, the first activity of application development might be business modeling. The introduction of a new computer application often requires changes to the manual business processes and the way the business is organized. If this is the case, business modeling is a required activity before requirements gathering.

Table 1.3   Probability of Project Failure

Function Points	Probability of Termination Prior to Completion
100	6%
1,000	17%
10,000	45%
100,000	80%

Reprinted with permission. *Source:* Jones, C., *Applied Software Measurement: Assuring Productivity and Quality*, Second ed. McGraw Hill, 1996.

Software development efforts fail much more often than they should. They fail in very high percentages. The bigger they are, the more often they seem to fall.

Capers Jones, founder of Software Productivity Research and metrics guru of the software industry, has done much interesting work on projects that fail. Table 1.3 shows that large projects fail in large numbers and small systems fail in small numbers.

The more complex the system, the larger the effort; the larger the effort, the more likely it is to fail. The major difference between developing systems 20 years ago and doing it today is that change is much more pervasive now. Changes to business processes and rules, user personnel, and technology make application development seem like trying to land a Frisbee on top of the head of a wild dog. The moving targets of requirements, tools, staff, and skills can make life difficult under the bright spotlight of an ongoing software project. The frequency of change means that systems must be built differently than they were before. They must be flexible enough so that changes can be made on-the-fly to requirements, design, code, testing, staff, and processes. The iterative/incremental lifecycle can address these issues because it accepts that each activity must be repeated multiple times to accommodate change even after the subsequent activities have started.

Software systems are more complex than most other engineering projects human beings undertake, but does that mean we're destined to produce overdue, poor-quality systems that don't last? We believe there are steps the industry can take to reverse this trend. If we focus on the root problems in software development and address them with high-quality processes and tools, we can make a real difference in producing more successful, on-time software that is resilient to change throughout its lifetime. For example, object orientation, when applied correctly, can address many of the issues of flexibility and extensibility in design and code for computer systems. It can also lessen the problems where maintenance of changes in one area cripples another area. Automated test tools can help address the massive test effort associated with iterative/incremental development. But how do we address requirements?

1.4 The Challenges of Requirements Gathering

If requirements gathering were easy, we wouldn't need to write a book about it. Following are the main challenges that we've observed in the process.

1.4.1 Finding Out What the Users Need

Everyone knows how to do this: "If you want to know what they want, just go ask them." When referring to users of a computer system, though, this advice is not very sound. Users do not know what they want, because the question—what will you want in your new computer system?—is so complex that users can't be expected to answer it. There are too many variables.

Once you are using new business procedures

and

your job has changed

and

the business your company is in changes

and

you are learning a brand-new computer application

how would you like it to work?

Users have much more on their minds than your computer application, including their own day-to-day responsibilities. The struggle between users' current responsibilities and their involvement in shaping a new system is legendary. Steve McConnell, in his book *Rapid Development* (McConnell 1996), gives us a number of ways that users can inhibit the process of requirements gathering:

- Users don't understand what they want.
- Users won't commit to a set of written requirements.
- Users insist on new requirements after the cost and schedule have been fixed.
- Communication with users is slow.
- Users often do not participate in reviews or are incapable of doing so.
- Users are technically unsophisticated.
- Users don't understand the software development process.
- And the list continues.

This list makes users sound like some kind of beasts that rise from the muck to interfere with our quest to develop applications. Of course, they're not. There is simply a tug-of-war between what the users need to concentrate on currently and how you need them to participate in helping you develop the application.

One defense against the struggle for users' time and attention during requirements gathering is simply to concentrate on establishing relationships with your users. The stronger the personal relationships between the analysts and the users, the more likely it is that the users will make the time for questions, meetings, and debates.

Another defense is to work on the visibility of the project. If senior executives in the users' organizations are aware of the system implementation and are touting its importance, it is more likely that the profile of the application among your users will be high enough to encourage them to attend requirements sessions and interviews, and to participate. They need to know that this effort is not just going to be another flash in the pan. Finally, it's important to be respectful of their time. To create the fewest disturbances possible, batch your questions and interviews together.

1.4.2 Documenting Users' Needs

As we said earlier, documenting users' needs is called *requirements definition*. Creating this documentation and then confirming it with them is a difficult process. This book is largely dedicated to making this process easier and clearer for all parties.

The challenge of documenting requirements with traditional techniques is that there are often no real checks and balances. It is hard to tell whether a requirement has already been documented, perhaps in a different way or with a conflicting result. It is also hard to see what's missing.

1.4.3 Avoiding Premature Design Assumptions

Premature design assumptions tend to creep into every requirements specification, especially if they're prepared by designers-at-heart. This also tends to happen if the people gathering the requirements don't trust the designers and want to tell them how the system should be designed so that the designers won't mess it up. This tends to happen, in our experience, when the developers are off-site and removed from the requirements gatherers and users. It also happens when the requirements analysts do not trust the designers and developers to make the right decisions later.

1.4.4 Resolving Conflicting Requirements

If requirements, big and small, are listed one after another in a list, as we showed in Section 1.1, there can be requirements in different places of the list that say opposite things. To combat this problem, you need a built-in mechanism to prevent these conflicts. You can use something with more structure than a list, and you can incorporate reviews when conflicts are identified.

1.4.5 Eliminating Redundant Requirements

Redundant requirements are not as bad as conflicts, but they can be confusing if they say *almost* the same thing, but not quite. They also add to the volume of the requirements, which can be its own problem.

1.4.6 Reducing Overwhelming Volume

The greater the volume of the requirements specification, the less likely it is that the development effort can succeed. The volume must be reduced in one or all of the following ways:

- Remove conflicts.
- Remove redundancy.
- Remove design assumptions.
- Find commonality among requirements and abstract them to the level that makes the most sense for the users.
- Separate functional from nonfunctional requirements.

1.4.7 Ensuring Requirements Traceability

When you're gathering requirements, the main thought that should be going through your mind is, Am I documenting things that will be understandable to the users and useful to the designers? Requirements must be traceable throughout the lifecycle of development. You should be able to ask any person in any role the questions in Table 1.4.

Table 1.4   Traceability Defined by Role

Role	Traceability
Analyst/designer	What requirements does this class on this class diagram relate to?
Developer	What requirements does the class you're programming relate to?
Tester	Exactly which requirements are you testing for when you execute this test case?
Maintenance programmer	What requirements have changed that require you to change the code that way?
Technical writer	What requirements relate to this section of the user manual?
Architect	What requirements define what this architectural component needs to do?

Role	Traceability
Data modeler	What requirements drove the design of this entity or database table/index?
Project manager	What requirements will be automated in working code in this iteration?

Unfortunately, these requirements traceability questions can rarely be answered in today's projects. But if they were, they would provide a solid audit trail for every activity in development and maintenance, and they would describe why the activities are being done. It would help prevent *developer goldplating*: the addition of system functionality that is not required by the users and therefore does not tie in with any documented requirements.

Automated tools are beginning to address the requirements traceability problem, but they're only part of the picture. We still need a little old-fashioned people management to maintain a *requirements audit trail*, which runs end-to-end throughout the lifetime of an application.

1.5 Issues with the Standard Approaches

Not only are there issues with the documentation typically produced during requirements gathering (the requirements list), but also there are often issues in the way the documentation is produced. This section looks at several common methods that can be used to bring together requirements for an application.

1.5.1 User Interviews

Obviously, conducting user interviews is necessary when you're building a requirements specification. A user interview normally focuses on users talking about how they do their job now, how they expect it will change after the system goes into production, and the typical problems they encounter with the current process. The requirements analyst is usually writing madly, trying to keep up with the users' remarks and trying to think of the next question to ask.

Often, when one interview with one user is complete and the next user is being interviewed, requirements analysts notice that the two people have conflicting views on the same process or business rule. Then, when people at various levels of management are interviewed, the playing field becomes even more interesting. Conflicting views become a multidimensional puzzle, with pieces that change their shape as the game proceeds. The question might arise in the analyst's mind, How can this company (or department) stay in business and continue to be profitable if no one can agree on how things are run? The answer is that the level of detail required to build a computer application is greater than the level of detail needed to run a business successfully. It is the only possible answer, given our experience with numerous user departments that ran perfectly well even though every employee gives different answers to the same questions.

1.5.2 Joint Requirements Planning Sessions

Joint requirements planning (JRP) sessions are similar to conducting all the user interviews at the same time in the same room. All the people who will influence the direction of the application are brought to one place and give their input into what the system will do. A facilitator leads the group to make sure things don't get out of hand, and a scribe makes sure everything gets documented, usually using a projector and diagramming software.

A JRP is similar in structure to a joint application design (JAD) session except that the focus is different. JAD sessions are focused on *how* the system will work, whereas JRP sessions are focused only on *what* the system will do. But the processes are similar.

The people involved in JRP sessions are key representatives from a variety of interested groups, or *stakeholders*: users, user management, operations, executives, regulatory agencies (IRS, SEC, and so on), maintenance programming, and so forth. During the JRP session, high-level topics, such as critical success factors and strategic opportunities, are the first agenda items. Then the application's functional and nonfunctional requirements are identified, documented, and prioritized in the presence of everyone.

*The JRP session provides an opportunity to get input from
a number of stakeholders at the same time.*

JRP sessions are valuable and can be significant timesavers for the requirements team. As hard as it is to get all the interested parties into one room (preferably off-site), it can be even harder to schedule time with each individual, given other distractions, interruptions, and priorities.

Our main issue with JRP is the document produced. In most cases, the document is a contract-style list of requirements—and you know how we feel about requirements lists.

An all-encompassing resource for successful JRPs is Ellen Gottesdiener's book *Requirements by Collaboration: Workshops for Defining Needs* (Addison-Wesley, 2002).

1.5.3 Contract-Style Requirements Lists

The requirements list has its problems. In most other areas of the software development lifecycle, we have evolved the documentation into effective diagrams along with text that is elegantly structured and useful. Requirements have lagged behind this trend. The requirements list must be replaced by something with more structure and more relevance to users and designers alike. We suggest that use cases, use case diagrams, and business rules replace the traditional requirements list.

Table 1.5 shows another example of a requirements list that needs to be improved. We have a few comments beside each requirement, but please feel free to add your own insights.

Table 1.5   More Requirements

Requirement	Comment
The system will support client inquiries from four access points: in person, paper-based mail, voice communication, and electronic communication (Internet, dial-up, and LAN/WAN).	Four access points are how; we should focus instead on who needs access from where.
The telephone system must be able to support an 800 number system.	An 800 number? Can't use 888 or 877? Again, what's missing is who needs what kind of access from where.
The telephone system must be able to handle 97,000 calls per year and must allow for a growth rate of 15 percent annually. Of these calls it is estimated that 19 percent will be responded to in an automated manner and 81 percent will be routed to call center staff for response. Fifty percent of the calls can be processed without reference to the electronic copy of the paper file, and approximately 50 percent will require access to the system files.	Valuable statistics; this one is actually pretty good.

continues

Table 1.5 *continued*

Requirement	Comment
For the calls that require access to system information, response times for the electronic files must be less than 20 seconds for the first image located on the optical disk, less than 3 seconds for electronic images on a server, and less than 1 second for data files.	Starts out nicely until we mention "optical disk," which is a design assumption. The response times would be good nonfunctional requirements if they weren't about a design assumption.
The telephone system must be able to support voice recognition of menu selections, touch-tone menu selections, and default to a human operator. The telephone menu will sequence caller choices in order of most frequently requested information to the least requested.	Pretty good one. Can you find anything wrong?
The telephone system must be able to provide a voice response menu going from a general menu to a secondary menu.	This seems to be trying to provide a dumb designer with some pretty obvious advice.
The system must allow for the caller to provide address information through a digital recording and to indicate whether it is permanent.	"Through a digital recording"? Who says? This is a design assumption.
The system must allow for the caller to provide address information through voice recognition and to indicate whether it is permanent.	Sound familiar? (It's redundant.)
The telephone system must be able to store and maintain processor IDs and personal identification numbers to identify callers and to route calls properly to the appropriate internal response telephone.	Simplify it: "The system must be able to identify callers and route calls to the appropriate internal response telephone."
The telephone system must be able to inform callers of the anticipated wait time based on the number of calls, average duration of calls, and number of calls ahead of them.	Great!

Requirement	Comment
The journal will contain entries for key events that have occurred within the administration of an individual's account. The system will capture date, processor ID, and key event description. The system will store pointers to images that are associated with a journal entry as well as key data system screens that contain more information regarding the entry.	This is a design for the journal. Why have it? What is its purpose?
If an individual double-clicks on an event in a member's journal, the system will display the electronic information and the images associated with the event.	Double-click is a user interface assumption.
The system will restrict options on the information bar by processor function. When an icon is clicked, the screen represented by the icon will be displayed and the system will display appropriate participant information.	This one has lots of user interface assumptions.

1.5.4 Prototypes

The prototype wave hit software development in the mid-1980s as fourth-generation languages became popular and usable. *Prototypes* are mock-ups of the screens or windows of an application that allow users to visualize the application that isn't yet constructed. Prototypes help the users get an idea of what the system will look like, and the users can easily decide which changes are necessary without waiting until after the system is built. When this approach was introduced, the results were astounding. Improvements in communication between user groups and developers were often the result of using prototypes. Early changes to screen designs helped set the stage for fewer changes later and reduced overall costs dramatically.

However, there are issues with prototypes. Users with detail-oriented minds pay more attention to the details of the screens than to the essence of what the prototype is meant to communicate. Executives, once they see the prototype, have a hard time understanding why it will take another year or two to build a system that looks as if it is already built. And some designers feel compelled to use the patched-together prototype code in the real system because they're afraid to throw any code away.

Prototypes will always be a part of systems development. But they cannot be the one and only requirements specification. They contain too much user interface design (which can be distracting to users and designers), and they imply that more of the system is built than is actually completed. They represent only the front end of the system—the presentation. The business rules are not usually represented unless the prototype is fully functional, and this means that a lot of effort must go into the prototype. Prototypes should be used for what they are best at: user interface specification. This means that perhaps prototypes should come along a little later than the bulk of the requirements work. Iterative/incremental lifecycles often reduce the need for prototypes, since the real application is available to be viewed, commented on, and changed as it is developed (see Chapter 7).

1.6 Those Troublesome Requirements

The traditional tools and techniques used for gathering requirements have not served us well. We usually get ahead of ourselves and start embedding design into our requirements specifications. We spend either too little or too much effort. We create prototypes that are helpful but are also distracting, and we create contract-style requirements lists that are difficult to use and don't provide any checks or balances. There must be a better way.

2

Moving to Use Cases

The computer industry has struggled to find a way to represent functionality to users. We have always tended to produce what we're comfortable with: diagrams and specifications that are loaded with terminology and notation that looks a lot more like computer code than anything a user would understand. The traditional modes of expressing functionality to users early in the lifecycle are as follows:

- Requirements specifications
- Functional decompositions
- Data-flow diagrams (DFDs)
- Entity-relationship diagrams (ERDs)
- Prototypes

Typically, requirements are specified in lists and expressed in terms of "the system shall." These lists are often grouped by functionality or subsystem. In such lists, it's easy to

The system shall . . .

inadvertently write duplicate or conflicting requirements, and it happens often. The requirements specification does not provide the users with a cohesive view of what the system will accomplish; it is merely an itemization of each of the various functions, as if the functions could be extracted and treated independently.

What requirements lists intend to provide is a comprehensive catalog of every function that the system should perform. Although it seems only natural to list these functions, it turns out that there are better ways to represent this information and provide a better structure than a list.

We recommend that requirements lists be dropped from the analyst's toolbox.

Functional decompositions are a remnant of the older analysis and design approaches.

Often in an attempt to "divide and conquer" a complex software application, a team will use a method called *functional decomposition.* This tool takes the major function of the system, the highest level "function" (also sometimes called *activity/process/action*) and breaks it down into subprocesses, and sub-subprocesses, and so on. Eventually, the processes are small enough to become a program (in computer programming terms). The highest-level function is usually called "Process Insurance Policy," "Process Requisition," or "Process" whatever.

This approach has been abandoned in the software industry for several reasons. First, it is tightly linked to structured systems development, meaning COBOL programs and mainframes. It is not usable for an application that will be Web-based or object-oriented once it is coded. Second, by dividing and conquering using "processes" it is easy to lose the connection to the "things" that we care about, the entities that become "objects" or "classes" in analysis and design. And, as we review later in section 4.3.2, hierarchies of requirements are not desirable for a well-designed software application. And third, functional decomposition has proven it is not capable of handling the contemporary complexity of today's information systems.

DFDs are useful for technical people but tend to confuse users.

Dataflow diagrams (DFDs) help show a system as a set of groups of interacting processes. We consider them to represent the dynamic view of the system. The data *flows* from one process to another and then stops in a data store. External entities, such as an outside department or computer system, are referenced whenever they have involvement in the flow of data. Because DFDs focus on what happens inside the system, they are the main input into system design. In our experience, users seem to be confused by these diagrams because the line between system and user responsibility is fuzzy. DFDs also contain a lot more detail than users are prepared to wade through. Some of these details, such as how many data stores are used and what they store, do not concern the users at all.

As with requirements lists, we recommend that DFDs be dropped from the requirements analyst's toolbox. DFDs introduce many technical elements into the requirements picture that are not necessary at this point. DFDs can be replaced by use cases and class, sequence, statechart, and activity diagrams in the Unified Modeling Language (UML).

NOTE: DFDs can still be useful in design, particularly with non-object-oriented systems. Just don't consider them a requirements artifact.

Entity-relationship diagrams (ERDs) show how the data is stored in an application. They show details of entities, attributes, and relationships. This diagram can also be used to represent a logical data model and dictate the structure of a relational database. However, ERDs do nothing to show dynamic interaction, and they must always be used along with DFDs to

ERDs are critical for database design, but they are not meant for user consumption.

show a complete picture to the users. The difference between a dynamic type of expression (DFDs) and a static or persistent expression (ERDs) is irrelevant and confusing to users.

We recommend that ERDs, too, be dropped from the requirements analyst's toolbox. ERDs are still required if you want to create a logical data model after requirements have been gathered, but ERDs do not provide much meaning to users and seem foreign to them.

Prototypes were long held to be the elixir for good requirements capture, but now we realize that they can help much more with proof-of-concept tasks.

Prototypes give users a realistic demonstration of what a system will be able to do when it is completed. These mock-up versions of the system concentrate on the user interface and omit all or most of the background coding. Prototypes are greeted with enthusiasm by users because they help them understand the possibilities much better than do paper diagrams. However, users' enthusiasm is problematic because they immediately get caught up in the details of the user interface and the mock-up data. Soon, they are spending more time requesting button moves and color changes than they are spending focusing on the functionality. Prototypes also lead users to the misperception that the prototype *is* the system, and they become impatient when it takes weeks or months to develop the actual system. Prototypes also encourage the team to continue quick-and-dirty coding after actual system development begins, evolving the prototype into the final system.

We recommend that prototypes no longer be used as a requirements tool. Instead, they should be used to support use cases and the business rules catalog, which become the central focus of the requirements phase.

Traditional requirements specifications are often never used again after they are produced. DFDs and ERDs are useful for moving into programming and database design, but they do not mean much to users. Prototypes are meaningful to users, but they encourage them to concentrate on the details of user interface implementation and not on the requirements of the system. What's needed is a new medium between users and system designers.

2.1 It's All About Interactions

Clearly, the combination of artifacts produced in our projects contains a lot of information. However, it may be that they contain too much information. What if the diagrams were to concentrate on the requirements of the system from the users' perspectives? The questions is then, What do the users see?

Users view computer systems as *black boxes*. This term implies that the perspective of the application is concerned only with what goes in and what comes out. The inner workings are not important to the black-box perspective. Requirements documentation that puts everything in the context of "going in" and "coming out" has more relevance to the users who study it.

When we talk about "going in" and "coming out," we're talking about interactions. Interactions between the users and the computer system are what really matter in requirements gathering. For example, it is important that a user wants to enter numbers in timesheets and have the system print checks. But it is not important to the user that those timesheets go through 18 specific processes before the checks are produced. That's design. The users care only that the checks are produced and that they're right.

For an IT specialist, grasping this concept is very tough. We have strong tendencies to jump into the *how* before we've defined the *what*. We're typically advised not to get too detailed. But this is not quite accurate. The *what* can become very detailed. For example,

Users care about what goes in and what comes out, as in a black box.

the definition of printing the checks "right," in our example, could be very detailed. Information about what the system should do with calculating weekly pay based on a yearly salary, handling hourly employees, dealing with overtime, and incorporating raises at the right time can be excruciatingly detailed. However, the focus must remain on the *what* and not drift into the *how*.

Use cases are a tool that can show the *what* exclusively. DFDs, ERDs, and prototypes include *what* and *how* in their perspectives, and that can confuse users. For this reason, we recommend that use cases be the primary tool for requirements gathering.

The Origin of Use Cases

Use cases were introduced to the IT world by Ivar Jacobson (1992) and his team at Ericsson in Sweden. Their book, *Object-Oriented Software Engineering* took the computing industry by storm and use cases have been increasing in popularity ever since. Jacobson included use cases as part of an overall system development lifecycle methodology called *Objectory*, which he marketed as a product and built a company around. Later, Jacobson's Objectory company and methodology were purchased by Rational Software, and Objectory, with its use cases, became part of the Rational Unified Process (Jacobson 1999). We owe a lot to Jacobson, and this book uses many of his ideas in the definition of use cases. Before Jacobson, various ideas about stories and scenarios as requirements were introduced by Meilir Page-Jones, Rebecca Wirfs-Brock, and others. Where we can add to the ideas of these industry giants is in the practical application of use cases to solve the requirements problem. As consultants and practitioners, we have worked with use cases on the job for many years, and we understand the good and bad points of them. In this book, we have attempted to improve upon use cases, without changing them fundamentally, but instead by surrounding them with other artifacts and helpful hints to help create a more complete requirements toolset.

2.2 The Unified Modeling Language

Introducing…the Unified Modeling Language!

Use cases aren't a phenomenon unto themselves. They are part of a comprehensive language called the Unified Modeling Language, or UML. This language was brought into existence in January 1997 and has subsequently been adopted as a standard by the Object Management Group (OMG), an industry consortium.

The UML is a *notation*: a way to document system specifications. It is not a methodology, it is a language. A notation simply tells you how to structure your system documentation. It provides the nomenclature of the diagrams and specifications that you produce. A *methodology*, by contrast, consists of a step-by-step guide to building a system. Methodologies are much more complex and contentious. The UML is not dependent on a particular methodology, nor do methodologies need to be contingent on the UML. The UML requires only that the computer system being built has object-oriented components. In fact, several of the UML diagrams, including use cases, can be used for systems that are not based on object orientation. Methodologies that work with the UML include the Rational Unified Process, the Object Modeling Technique, the Booch method, Objectory, Schlaer-Mellor, FUSION, OPEN, and many others.

Of course, the UML did not appear magically from outer space. It was the result of collaborations between three famous object-oriented methodologists: Grady Booch, James Rumbaugh, and Ivar Jacobson (1999). The "Three Amigos," as they are called, combined their own modeling notations and also got plenty of ideas and unanimous buy-in from every other major methodologist in the industry. Through their efforts, the computer industry has a common language,[1] or notation, with which to specify object-oriented systems—something this industry has never before experienced.

---

1. There is at least one other notation that we are aware of that is in competition with the UML. It is called OML or OPEN Modeling Language. The OML is part of a methodology called OPEN, or Object-Oriented Process, Environment, and Notation. OPEN and OML are being championed by Donald Firesmith, Brian Henderson-Sellers, Ian Graham, and Meilir Page-Jones—an impressive roster to say the least. OML is billed as a "superset of the UML," however, it is likely to serve only as a set of recommendations to the OMG for future enhancements to the UML. We do not expect it to compete with the UML directly. SEE: http://www.markv.com/OPEN/

The UML is composed of nine diagrams.

- Use case diagram
- Sequence diagram
- Collaboration diagram
- Statechart diagram
- Activity diagram
- Class diagram
- Object diagram
- Component diagram
- Deployment diagram

These diagrams, used properly within the context of a solid methodology, can convey all the necessary views of a computer system and can provide the basis for constructing, configuring, and deploying the system. There are many interdependencies between these diagrams. Construction on one type of diagram means changes to others. Software tools[2] can help manage these interdependencies. The UML lends itself well to automated analysis and design tools and also provides many possibilities for generating code from design documentation and for *reverse engineering (creating design from code)*.

The UML is a well-thought-out notation that serves analysts, designers, and architects. It is comprehensive, especially when compared with earlier object-oriented notations. It is also the new standard for object-oriented systems notation, and that's the best reason of all to use it for all your documentation needs. But remember—to be successful on your project, you must choose and implement a methodology along with the UML. Adopting the UML by itself is not enough.

This book is dedicated to explaining how use cases can solve problems in requirements gathering. It is not meant to provide a tutorial for the UML, but it is important that you understand how use cases fit into the context of the UML. Books on the UML include the following:

- *The Unified Modeling Language Reference Manual* (by James Rumbaugh, Ivar Jacobson, Grady Booch), Addison Wesley, 1998
- *Applying UML and Patterns* (by Craig Larman), Prentice-Hall PTR, 2001
- *The Unified Modeling Language User Guide* (by Grady Booch, James Rumbaugh, Ivar Jacobson), Addison Wesley, 1999

2.2.1 Nine Diagrams

In the following sections we take a look at the nine UML diagrams in some detail.

---

2. Our favorite analysis and design tools that support the UML are MagicDraw UML, ArgoUML (an open source tool), and Rational Rose.

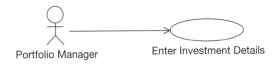

Figure 2.1   *UML Use Case Diagram*

2.2.1.1 Use Case Diagram

Figure 2.1 shows an example of a *use case diagram.*

Use cases, obviously, are a focus of this book. They are the driver for the rest of the diagrams. Although the UML is not a methodology and therefore does not prescribe steps, it makes the assumption that you diagram use cases before you start the other diagrams. Use cases form the basis of how the system interacts with the outside forces around it: users/actors, other systems, and other factors (date/time, special environmental conditions, and so on).

Use cases are text descriptions of the interaction between some outside actors and the computer system. Use case diagrams are graphical depictions of the relationships between actors and use cases and between a use case and another use case.

Use cases and use case diagrams should be documents that users can interpret easily. They are meant to be written in "user language," devoid of any "objectspeak" or implementation details. Inside each use case is a nice little package of requirements that effectively drives the rest of the system development process.

Use cases drive not only requirements gathering but also the entire software development cycle. Several methodologies, including the popular Rational Unified Process (RUP), are use-case-driven. Use cases have the simplicity to represent a computer system's essence, and yet they have the power to drive the entire methodology, in the process helping to solve problems such as requirements traceability.

2.2.1.2 Sequence and Collaboration Diagrams

Sequence diagrams (Figure 2.2) and *collaboration* diagrams (Figure 2.3) show the internal workings of a use case scenario (see Section 2.3.1.4). They present a dynamic view of a system, showing how messages pass between objects to satisfy a use case.

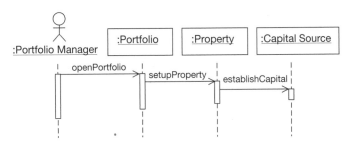

Figure 2.2   *UML Sequence Diagram*

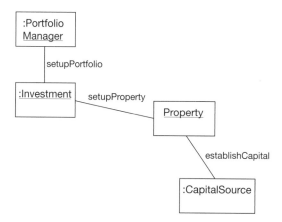

Figure 2.3   *UML Collaboration Diagram*

Collaboration diagrams have the same function as sequence diagrams, but sequence diagrams are geared toward simple, linear interactions, whereas collaboration diagrams are geared toward more complex interactions such as multithreaded or conditional messaging.

2.2.1.3 State and Activity Diagrams

State and *activity* diagrams are also part of the dynamic view of a system. In contrast to sequence and collaboration diagrams, statecharts and activity diagrams concentrate on transition from one state to another rather than on the messages that pass between objects. State diagrams (Figure 2.4) are generally used for simpler state transition views and activity diagrams (Figure 2.5) are used for more complex views.

2.2.1.4 Class and Object Diagrams

Although the previous diagrams show the dynamic view of a computer system, *class* diagrams are geared toward the static view. Class diagrams (Figure 2.6) show how classes are constructed and list their names, attributes, and operations. They also show how classes are related to one another statically, using associations such as generalization and aggregation.

Object diagrams show the relationships among *objects*, which are the instances created at runtime from the class templates. The structure of an object diagram is similar to that of a class diagram except that the focus is on the runtime instantiations of the classes.

2.2.1.5 Component Diagram

Component diagrams (Figure 2.7) help move the system from a collection of fine-grained objects to a collection of coarser-grained components, and they help show how these components relate to one another.

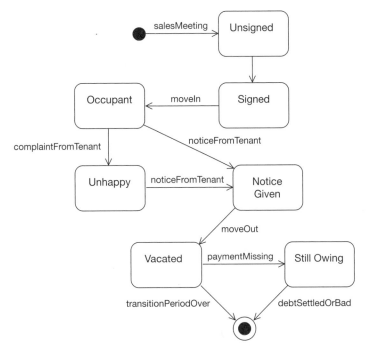

Figure 2.4 *UML State Diagram*

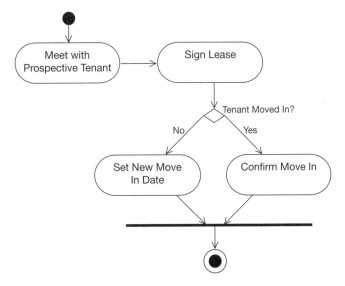

Figure 2.5 *UML Activity Diagram*

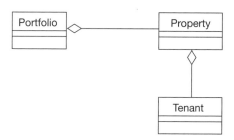

Figure 2.6   *UML Class Diagram*

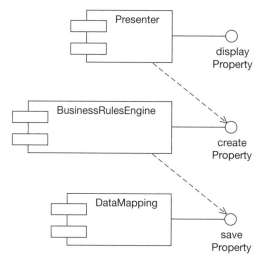

Figure 2.7   *UML Component Diagram*

2.2.1.6 Deployment Diagram

Deployment diagrams (Figure 2.8) show how components of the system will be deployed to different physical nodes, or machines, in the production environment.

2.2.1.7 Packages

Another convenient UML mechanism is the package metaphor. *Packages* are a way to hide complexity. They can be used with use cases, classes, components, or deployment nodes. For more information on packages, see *The Unified Modeling Language User Guide* (Booch 1999). Figure 2.9 shows a UML package diagram.

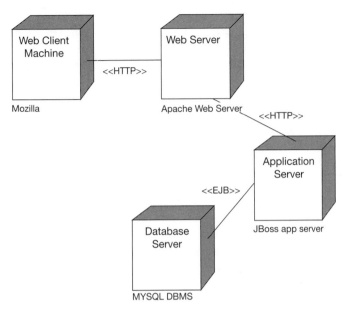

Figure 2.8   *UML Deployment Diagram*

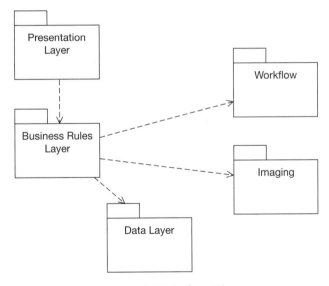

Figure 2.9   *UML Package Diagram*

2.2.2 Extending the UML with Stereotyping

We hope that the UML will last for years and years. But how can a modeling language last in the computer field, where the only constant is change? And how can this general-purpose language be useful for each specific situation, when circumstances may require new types of elements or diagrams?

The UML addresses these issues with a feature called *stereotypes*. Stereotyping lets you *extend* the UML to represent new types of abstractions or concepts. Stereotyping is extremely powerful and enables you to customize the UML for your project. It also means that the UML will not go out of date as quickly as most modeling languages because it can be adapted to handle the changes it faces.

What are stereotypes? Stereotypes are a way to classify UML building blocks (or elements) in a more specific way to add meaning to a diagram. Stereotypes let you group characteristics that are common among several use cases, for example, and thereby change the specification of a use case to a more specialized form, perhaps a mission-critical use case. The *mission critical* stereotype might specify that a requirement of all use cases of this stereotype is that they respond to the actor within three seconds on each interaction.

In addition to use cases, all other UML elements—components, nodes, associations, and objects—can be stereotyped. The most common UML element to be stereotyped is classes.

The UML has several built-in stereotypes. For example, on the use case diagram, associations between use cases are stereotyped as *includes* or *extends* to show special kinds of associations that are unique to the use case diagram.

This book uses several kinds of stereotypes to increase the relevance of use cases to requirements gathering. We discuss these stereotypes in later chapters.

Stereotypes can be introduced by anyone who uses the UML, including individual practitioners. For the purposes of this book, we use stereotyping to help clarify the concepts we are introducing. (You can read more about our new stereotypes in Section 3.8.2.)

In the sample use case diagram in Figure 2.10, the *Enter Tenant Details* use case is classified with the stereotype *mission critical*. This means that all use cases marked with this stereotype must meet certain criteria; in this case, the transaction must be secure and must have less than a ten-second response time. The definition for *mission critical* might be specified in a separate document that addresses all stereotypes.

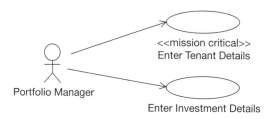

Figure 2.10   UML Stereotypes

2.3 Introducing Use Cases, Use Case Diagrams, and Scenarios

DEFINITION: A **use case** represents a series of interactions between an outside entity and the system, which ends by providing business value.

Part of our solution to the requirements-gathering problem is to deploy use cases, a deceptively simple tool that examines a computer system by expressing the interactions between the system and its environment: what goes in and what comes out. This sounds simple, but in practice it becomes very difficult. In our experience, systems professionals have an extremely hard time producing use cases that mean anything to the users. Systems people are used to dealing with systems as white boxes, not black boxes, and are focused on the *how*. Users see only the black box: the *what*.

In the book *Zen and the Art of Motorcycle Maintenance*, Robert Pirsig (1994) uses historical terms to describe differing views of a motorcycle: the *classic* view and the *romantic* view. The classic view sees a motorcycle in terms of its subsystems: power train, braking, steering, safety, and so on. The romantic view sees the motorcycle as what it can do for the rider: speed up, slow down, weave through traffic, avoid accidents, and so forth. Each view sees exactly the same motorcycle, but they see it from much different perspectives.

Two people see a motorcycle in two ways: as the subsystems that make up the bike and as the things a person can do with the bike.

Use cases in the requirements activity see the system from the romantic view. They are concerned only with what the system can do for the users. This makes them extremely effective for conveying information to users because they cut out all classic viewpoints and boil down the requirements to the barest essentials.

To apply use cases effectively to the requirements-gathering process, you need to understand the goals of use cases, which are discussed in the next section. Use cases are simple in structure, but preparing them correctly is difficult. This is often the case with simple representations of complex things. In the following subsections, we explore the notation of the use case and how it fits in with the rest of the UML.

2.3.1 The Goals of Use Cases

2.3.1.1 Interactions That Provide Value to Actors

Use cases are meant to show the interactions between the system and the entities external *to the system*. External entities, or actors, include users, other computer systems, or external events, such as reaching a specific date or time. Each interaction should provide something of value to the external entity. If it does not, it should contribute directly to a value provided to an external entity that does not participate in the interaction. For example, a management information system may not provide value to the clerk who keys in volumes of data, but the data contributes directly to the manager, who uses the data to make business decisions. Similarly, a production accounting system may gather information from a metering system but actually provide the value to another actor, perhaps a general ledger system. When the interaction occurs between the system and an external event such as date/time, the external event does not gain a value from the interaction; nevertheless, some other external entity should benefit from the interaction.

2.3.1.2 No Implementation-Specific Language

As mentioned previously, use cases are black-box representations, and this means that use cases do not include any *implementation-specific language*. As the use case author, you avoid using implementation-specific language by not making any assumptions about how this use case is realized in program code or the user interface. Table 2.1 provides examples of implementation-specific language and our suggestions for improving it.

Be careful about using implementation-specific terms in these areas:

- Specific people (instead of roles)
- Specific departments in the organization
- User interface widgets (buttons, menu navigation, hardware references)
- Assumptions about where the work is being done physically
- IF-THEN-ELSE statements in use case text
- Pseudocode in use case text
- The use of any kind of constraint language in use case text (such as Object Constraint Language [OCL])

Hand in hand with the rejection of implementation-specific language, use cases should be written in the users' vocabulary. All data items and interactions should be termed and phrased using the same language that the users adopt to describe their jobs.

Table 2.1   Removing Implementation-Specific Language

Don't	Do	Assumptions Removed
The clerk pushes the OK button.	The clerk signifies completion of the transaction.	User interface button
The account holder folds the envelope with the cash or check and deposit slip and places it inside the slot on the automated teller machine (ATM).	The account holder provides the deposit, including cash, check, and deposit summary data.	Envelope, deposit slip, slot, ATM
The customers use the mouse to click on their part selection for the zip code they specified in the pull-down box and then click on the hyperlink to the Order Finalization Web page.	The customer chooses a part from a list of available parts in the specified zip code.	Mouse clicks, pull-down box, hyperlink, Web page, navigation from one page to another

We call use cases that have no implementation references *context-free* use cases. It means that we can apply these use cases to any context—technical, implementation, user interface, workflow, and so forth—and they will still be perfectly applicable.

Sometimes, implementation-specific language is OK. Having stated firmly that you should never put implementation-specific details in use cases, now let's discuss when you should do it: when they are being produced or refined outside the boundaries of requirements gathering. Because use cases drive the whole lifecycle, it is reasonable to assume that they are modified throughout the lifecycle. In fact, use cases become increasingly implementation-specific as time goes on, reflecting the work being done at the time. Another term for implementation-specific, in this context, is *real*. The term *real use cases* comes from Larry Constantine (1999) and is documented in Craig Larman's book (2002). Any use cases that reflect the requirements view should be saved separately, but they can also become input to use cases that help manage the work of design, construction, testing, and architecture.

2.3.1.3 User-Appropriate Level of Detail

As you proceed through requirements gathering, use cases go from being general to being detailed. As IT professionals, we tend to migrate to the details quickly. It is important to at least start at a general level before jumping to the details. Keep in mind that use cases should always be in the users' vocabulary. This may help you keep to a suitable level of detail.

2.3.1.4 User-Appropriate Volume

At the Object-Oriented Programming System, Languages, and Applications (OOPSLA) conference in 1996, Ivar Jacobson said that a very large system should have no more than 70 to 80 use cases. He stated that he couldn't imagine a system so large it would require 100 use cases. Sound impossible? This means that most systems would have perhaps 20 to 50 use cases, and some small systems even fewer. Debbie Ard, a business analyst friend of ours, has decided that every reasonably large application seems to have 28 use cases! That is a great number to shoot for; it is an easy set of use cases to understand and relate to.

We have found that if we use good judgment, it is not only possible but also extremely wise to keep the number of use cases very small. In producing such a small number of use cases for functionality so grand, the analysts and users are forced to abstract the activities of the system until they truly represent what the system must accomplish. After the distractions and assumptions are pulled out, two processes that may seem to be unique begin to merge, and a better abstraction results.

Please note that we refer to the number of use cases and not the number of scenarios. *Scenarios* are individual instances of use cases that traverse a specific path using specific data. There can be a large number of scenarios, depending on how detailed the testing effort becomes or how much confusion exists between users and requirements analysts.

Remember that each use case represents a fairly abstract interaction between actor and system. The individual paths through the use case, shown in the Alternative Path and Exception Path sections in the use case template (discussed in Section 2.3.3), form the basis for the detailed processing that usually requires volumes of documentation to represent.

2.3.2 How Use Case Diagrams Show Relationships

Use cases are text documents. To show two kinds of relationships—those between use cases and those between use cases and actors—we employ use case diagrams. As with all UML diagrams, use case diagrams have specific rules about notation. The following subsections explain these rules.

2.3.2.1 Actors and Roles

DEFINITION: An actor is an outside entity that interacts with the system.

Use cases never initiate actions on their own. The initiator of all interactions is the actor: something outside the computer application. Actors can be people, other computer systems, or something more abstract, such as a specific date and time. Actors shown on the use

The use case actor?

case diagram should be those that interact directly with the system or are influenced directly by the system.

It is often hard to decide which actors to show on a use case diagram. For example, when a supplier provides an invoice to a company clerk and the clerk enters the invoice into the system, should the supplier be included in the diagram? If the supplier is shown, it is called a *secondary* actor. Our rule is that the supplier should be shown in the diagram if the supplier's behavior impacts the system in any way. For example, if a supplier sends a shipment late and that changes how the system reacts, then the supplier should be in the diagram.

Other computer systems can also be actors. For example, when your system feeds postings to a general ledger system, that general ledger system becomes an actor in your use case diagram. Similarly, if other systems feed your system, they should also appear in your diagrams. A trigger of some sort can also be an actor. For example, if a system goes into action when a certain date or time is reached, such as 7:00 PM on the last workday of the month, then the date/time becomes the actor. Similarly, if a system is initiated by a condition of its environment, such as the pressure in a natural gas pipeline increasing above a certain level, then the pressure in the pipeline becomes the actor. However, the system in scope for your project can never be an actor. If actors are outside the boundaries of your system, by definition, the system you are building cannot be outside the scope!

Actors are external to the system and outside its responsibility. It might be helpful to treat each actor as an *assumption*. You assume that the actor is out of scope and that the system will interact with it but not automate it.

Actors can be treated as use cases when analysts begin looking at the use cases to start building an object model. Actors may influence how the classes are constructed; in fact, they themselves may become classes. Therefore, it makes sense to take care in creating the right actor to interact with the use cases. (We talk about how actors in use cases influence security in Chapter 8.)

Interactions between actors and use cases are shown with a straight, unbroken line with no arrows. It is not customary to label these lines. The description of what is behind these lines is what constitutes the Basic Course of Events section in the use case text.

Good actor names are quite specific but are not linked to organizational positions or certain users.

When to Show Secondary Actors

You should show secondary actors on use case diagrams when the specific actions of the secondary actor have an effect on the responses the application provides. Another rule of thumb is to make early judgments about whether the data regarding this secondary actor will be stored in the system in any way.

Role Names

You may notice that there are names at the actor ends of the arrows in the use case diagram examples. These are *role names*. Role names are useful when the association between an actor and a use case needs information beyond the fact that they interact. In this example, these associations are special because the actors are only *observers*. This role must be defined according to its implications. Perhaps they have read-only access to some data. This information is captured now, at requirements time, and is useful later in design.

2.3.2.2 Associations

Associations can exist between an actor and a use case, between use cases, and between actors. Let's examine each type of association.

Generalization

Generalization is a concept that is borrowed from the object-oriented world. When several use cases, for example, have something in common that can be abstracted into another, higher-level use case, they are said to be generalized.

Figure 2.11 shows two *subactors* being generalized into a *superactor*. Two types of representatives—customer and field—have behavior or attributes in common that are described under the service representative superactor. This type of generalization of actors should be done for one of two reasons.

- The superactors and subactors all have interactions with the use cases.
- There is considerable description that is common between the two subactors that would otherwise be duplicated.

The superactor should interact with use cases when all its subactors interact the same way with use cases. The subactors should interact with use cases when their individual interactions differ from that of the superactor.

Use cases can also be generalized using the same notation, but it is not used very often. We usually create one use case diagram that contains nothing but the actor generalizations.

Extend

Use case associations stereotyped as *<<extend>>* indicate a relationship in which a special use case (the blunt side of the association) extends an original use case (the sharp side of the association). This is useful when certain special cases would clutter up the original use case.

In Figure 2.12, the use case *Schedule Recurring Customer Appointment* extends the functionality of *Schedule Customer Appointment*. This means that it changes the interaction with the actor in some tangible way that would be cumbersome to include in the original use cases. For example, the actor might need to input the number of recurring appointments or the date that appointments should stop recurring. This particular interaction would not occur in the original use case.

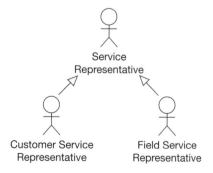

Figure 2.11   *Customer and Field Representative Generalized as Service Representative*

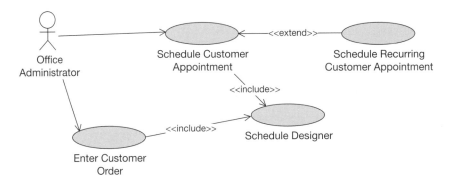

Figure 2.12   *Include and Extend Notation*

The *extending* use case (the blunt side of the arrow) is the special case of the *extended* use case (the sharp side of the arrow), and therefore the *extending* use case would not exist without the *extended* use case.

Include

The *<<include>>* association stereotype allows use case designers to avoid duplicating steps across multiple use cases. You deploy it as a reuse strategy for use case text instead of cutting and pasting steps into multiple use case documents.

In Figure 2.12, *Enter Costume Order*, *Schedule Customer Appointment*, and *Enter Uniform Order* have some similar steps, which can be drawn out into a separate use case called *Schedule Designer*. There may be other pieces of these use cases that are common, and they, too, could become separate use cases with *include* associations back to the owning use cases.

Our frank advice about <<extend>> and <<include>> is this: **don't use them.** There are almost always ways to avoid using them, and the dangers of using them are so great that it is best to stay away. One instance where *<<extend>>* or *<<include>>* may be appropriate is where the use cases of an initial release of a product must be enhanced for a second release, and therefore the original use cases may be extended to add the new functionality.

2.3.3 The Use Case Template

Most of the UML elements are diagrams. A use case is actually a page or two of text representing each oval in the use case diagram.

You need a common template for use cases in a project. Figure 2.13 presents a sample template. Standardization on a template is more important than what the template itself looks like. You can use our template or the template supplied with the RUP. Or, best of all, you can create your own template that uniquely addresses the requirements of your organization. It is helpful, however, if the same template is used for all projects within an organization. We have these rules for creating good-quality templates.

Use Case Name:	
Iteration:	
Summary:	
Basic Course of Events:	
Alternative Paths:	
Exception Paths:	
Extension Points:	
Triggers:	
Assumptions:	
Preconditions:	
Postconditions:	
Related Business Rules:	
Author:	
Date:	

Figure 2.13 *A Sample Use Case Template*

- Make each section meaningful. For example, don't have a section for Goals and another one for Objectives. For use cases, these are probably variations of the same thing.
- Use as few sections as possible to accomplish the job. We found ourselves creating more and more boxes on our form, but if users are to use this template easily, the fewer boxes the better. Users like use case templates that allow them to speed-read when they are reviewing the documents, so organize the template with that in mind.
- Each use case will probably be a page or more of text. Give yourself plenty of space to work with and don't constrain your line length by having more than one column in a page. It will reduce readability.

2.3.3.1 Use Case Name

The use case name provides a unique identification. We prefer a unique identifier that is written in English. Long ID numbers tend to turn off users.

2.3.3.2 Iteration

Iteration relates to each of the three stages through which we see use cases progressing: Facade, Filled, and Focused (see Section 3.3). Each use case progresses through these iterations at its own pace.

2.3.3.3 Summary

In one or two sentences, describe the interaction that occurs in this use case. Try not to regurgitate the basic course of events. Remember that each section should add its own unique value. The summary section may provide some context that other sections don't contain.

2.3.3.4 Basic Course of Events

This is the meat of the use case. Describe the steps that the actors and the system go through to accomplish the goal of this use case. The actor always takes the first step, and then the system responds. This goes back and forth until the goal has been accomplished, with some value being provided to the actor.

The basic course of events represents the "simple, correct path" through the use case. This means that no errors or missteps occur, either by the actor or the system. It also means that it shows the most common path taken. For example, a retailer may find that 80 percent of all orders use purchase orders (POs), with only occasional cash, check, or credit card use. This means that the basic course of events should show the details of a PO without concern for the other types of payment.

Sometimes, courses of events are shown with separate columns for the actor's actions and the system's actions. This arrangement helps to show the interaction that occurs. However, it also makes the use case confusing if more than one actor is involved, something that may happen in some specialized cases (for details, see Section 2.3.2.1).

Although we state that use cases are text and not diagrams, we'd like to hedge that definition slightly. The structure, or template, of the use case is text. However, if some kind of picture helps the understanding of a use case, it should be included or attached to the use case. For example, it's quite acceptable to include a price schedule in table format. Furthermore, pictures of decision trees, calculations, flowcharts, or Petri nets are also quite acceptable either inside the use case or as attachments. Again, let the users' perspectives be your guide. If the users will understand the use case better with the pictures, include them.

2.3.3.5 Alternative Paths

The Alternative Paths section shows the less-common paths that need to be addressed. They include situations in which unusual types of processing occur. An alternative path would be taken when an uncommon condition occurs, such as the cash, check, or credit card payment mentioned previously.

A single use case often includes several types of alternatives. For example, the *Enter Sale* use case, which has different types of payment, may also contain alternatives relating to the type of customer, whether industrial or consumer. An industrial customer might have a standing account to which orders are collected and billed monthly, whereas walk-in consumer business is conducted with cash or credit card. Each alternative should indicate which step, in the basic course of events, is its starting point.

Alternative paths listed separately from a basic course of events allow you to avoid IF-THEN-ELSE structures. Users usually do not understand programming structures of any kind: IF-THEN-ELSE, DO-WHILE, TRY-CATCH, and so on.

Sometimes it is difficult to determine the most common alternative. It is a good rule of thumb to try to determine the statistics of use. If they are not available, choose the simplest interaction. If cash is the easiest, involving the least number of steps and verifications, then choose it as your basic course of events. The main objective is to avoid confusing the users by creating a use case that does not reflect their daily work because they seldom see that type of transaction. The Alternative Paths section is where the less common interactions are documented.

2.3.3.6 Exception Paths

Exception paths, like alternative paths, show uncommon processing. Exception paths, however, show the interactions that occur when an error happens.

For example, an exception path is taken when an actor enters an invalid date. The system provides an error message, and the actor reenters the date.

2.3.3.7 Extension Points

In Section 2.3.2.2 we talk about the *extend* relationship, an association between use cases. The *extend* relationship exists between two use cases when one use case provides an optional sequence of events that is included in the other use case. The extension points show the steps in a use case from which the extending use cases extend. As we said before, it is best to avoid extend and include if at all possible. However, in those few extenuating circumstances, we've allowed for them here.

2.3.3.8 Triggers

Triggers describe the entry criteria for the use case. They are a list of the conditions that you expect to be true when an actor begins a use case. Triggers may describe a business need or be time-related, or a trigger could be the completion of another use case. Triggers answer the question "When or why will the actors enter this use case?"

2.3.3.9 Assumptions

From the project manager's point of view, this is a critical section. It is here that you document the things that you assume to be true but that might not be true. For example, if you assume that the actor has access to a current pricing list (which is not in the scope of this system) and if this use case's interactions depend on that, mention it here.

2.3.3.10 Preconditions

List the preconditions of this interaction. Preconditions are things that must be in place before the interaction can occur. They are part of the contract between this use case and the outside world.

Preconditions relate to conditions outside the scope of this use case and the computer system being developed. An example of a precondition is that a ledger exists for the incoming transaction.

2.3.3.11 Postconditions

Postconditions, like preconditions, are part of the contract between this use case and the outside world. After this use case has been completed successfully, the postconditions are satisfied.

Postconditions should be independent of the alternative path taken inside the use case. However, they do not need to be so generic that they deal with what happens when there is an error, especially an error in the input from the actor. An example of a postcondition is that a transaction is posted successfully to a ledger.

2.3.3.12 Related Business Rules

Business rules are the written and unwritten rules that dictate how a company conducts its business. This section in the use case template allows you to document or to refer to business rules that relate to the requirements presented in the use case. We find it more convenient to reference business rules than to include their entire text. In Section 3.9 we describe a business rules catalog for this purpose.

2.3.3.13 Author

You were probably expecting to see Author and Date at the top of the template, but we put them at the bottom. The most critical information should be at the top, where it can be spotted and read quickly and easily. We have heard users remark that if they can't speed-read a use case, they want it rewritten. This makes good sense, and it should be a guiding principle for designing use case templates.

2.3.3.14 Date

The Date section contains the date the use case was originally written, with references to when it was completed at each iteration. Here's an example.

Facade complete	Jan 29, 2004
Filled complete	Feb 4, 2004
Focused complete	Feb 12, 2004

These descriptions relate to how the use case template works best for us in our projects. Feel free to make the use case template your own by adding, deleting, or changing sections or changing the way it's used. We ask only that you stick to the guiding principles mentioned at the beginning of this section.

2.3.4 Paths and Scenarios

Use cases cannot tell the whole story. They are not highly detailed, and there are not many of them. To focus on the detailed interactions, we require a different tool: scenarios. Use Case 2.2 is a sample scenario that details each of the use case's interactions.

Use Case Name:	Determine Benefits Eligibility for Enrollee
Use Case Steps:	1. This use case starts when the social worker enters the enrollee's name and employment situation. 2. This use case ends when the system responds with a determination of whether the enrollee is eligible for benefits and the financial extent of the benefits.
Alternative Path:	In step 1, if the enrollee has applied for benefits previously, based on the enrollee's own disclosure, the social worker enters the enrollee's name to search for his or her previous records.[a]

Use Case 2.2   *Enter Investment Details*

a. Let's say that there is a government regulation that the social worker is not allowed to look for previous applications unless the enrollee discloses such.

This example also demonstrates how we use the word *scenario*. In the world of requirements gathering, perhaps no term is as maligned as this one. As far as we know, there are at least three definitions of the term. For clarification, we provide each of the definitions in this section. We start with an extract of steps and alternatives from a simplified use case for a welfare application system. Then we put forth several contradicting definitions of what the scenarios would be given this use case.

1. Shauna Thompson navigates to the investment details area.
2. Investments are identified by a name and system assigned number, including the Senatorial Business Park, property number 0513.
3. Shauna selects the Senatorial Business Park from a system displayed list.
4. The system locates the investment; it retrieves the details and displays them.
5. Shauna enters the following identifying details of the investment:
   a. Name_Senatorial Business Park (already there)
   b. Location_547 Second Avenue, Park City WA 98077
   c. Category_Office
   d. Investment manager_Shauna selects Alfred Dunning.
6. Shauna enters the capital commitment schedule.
   e. Date (Feb 27, 2004), capital (cash), source (Edwards Investments), amount ($4M), estimate high ($4.5M), estimate low ($3.5M), notes (This deal must close before April 1, 2004).
7. Shauna has no other property records to enter.
8. Shauna has no free form notes.
9. Shauna has no other contract details to enter.

10. Shauna is satisfied with the changes, she commits them, and the system responds by checking that all mandatory information about a deal is entered.

Scenario Definition 1, The Alternative Path: Example of a Scenario

1. This scenario starts when the social worker determines that the enrollee has applied for benefits previously, based on the enrollee's own disclosure, and therefore enters the enrollee's name to search for his or her previous records.
2. The system responds with the enrollee's previous records, including the number of previous applications and the benefit eligibility results.
3. The social worker asks the enrollee whether he or she has applied previously for and/or received benefits through this agency. If the enrollee has applied previously for benefits, the social worker enters the enrollee's welfare recipient number or searches by name if the enrollee cannot supply the welfare recipient number.

Scenario Definition 2, The Instance

A scenario is a realization of a use case, meaning that it is one possible path (similar to scenario definition 1), but it also includes the specific data.
Example of Scenario

1. The social worker asks Edward Trueman if he has applied previously for and/or received benefits, and Mr. Trueman replies that he has applied previously.
2. The social worker provides Mr. Trueman's name as the search criterion.
3. The system provides Mr. Trueman's previous records, which state that he applied for benefits on December 9, 1997, and was determined to be ineligible on December 9, 1997, because of his current part-time employment status at Boeing Aerospace in the capacity of assembly line worker.

Scenario Definition 3, The Synonym

Scenario is a synonym for *use case* (which is a synonym for *script*). This is the way some methodologists who provided input into the UML, such as Peter Coad, identified their version of the use case.

If you choose definition 1 (the alternative path), there is no need for scenarios as separate artifacts because they merely restate what was listed more succinctly in the Alternative Paths section of the use case. If you choose definition 3 (the synonym), you do not require scenarios as separate artifacts because they *are* use cases.

Our view is that definition 2 (the instance) is the only definition that provides additional value. By including sample data, preferably taken from production files, you can prove effectively that a use case can handle that set of circumstances. Scenarios can be used in two places in the development lifecycle to prove that a use case reflects accurately what the users need it to do. First, they can be used during the requirements activity to provide immediate feedback to the users and analysts as to whether the use cases are accurate reflections of the users' needs. Second, they can be used during the testing activity to test whether the computer system reflects the requirements. This is only one way that use cases drive the rest of the lifecycle. We talk more about this in Chapter 8.

To summarize, scenarios are *instances* of use cases (complete with production data) that effectively test one path through a use case. They are meant to demonstrate whether a use case reflects accurately the needs of the users, using terms and examples that the users understand. Scenarios are a useful vehicle for testing the validity of use cases early in the lifecycle.

The Difference Between Exception Path and Alternative Path

Exception path and *alternative path* sound as if they're describing the same thing. However, they are worth differentiating. An exception path contains steps that execute if something goes wrong, such as an input from the actor that the system cannot handle or a condition or series of conditions that occurs that are not part of the functionality. An example of an exception path is an actor keying in a record for a search and the record not being found.

An alternative path is actually much closer to the basic course of events because everything happens correctly (in other words, there are no errors); an alternative path simply is less likely to happen than the basic course of events. An example of an alternative path is the use of an unusual form of payment, such as the use of a credit card when a PO is more common.

When designing the use case template for your project, you may decide to lump exception and alternative paths together under one heading or to keep them separate. In our template, we separate them because we think it helps when producing scenarios. It is more important to generate scenarios, including a wide variety of alternative paths, than to worry about exceptions.

2.4 Use Cases Apply Here

Use cases apply to a wide range of activities and not only to requirements gathering. In this section we look at the application of use cases in a couple of areas that you might not have thought of. Also, in Chapter 8 we show how use cases apply to other activities in the lifecycle.

2.4.1 Use Cases for Inquiry-Only Systems

Use cases make sense for any system that has interactions with the outside world. It is not outrageous to say that any computer system should interact with the outside world. The most common application of use cases occurs in transaction-processing systems. However, inquiry-only systems, such as data warehouses, are also good candidates for use case requirements gathering.

There are a few caveats. Inquiry-only use cases are usually more abstract than transaction-processing use cases. Data warehouses are built to offer users flexible interfaces that can provide multiple views of volumes of data. This flexibility means that the users' actual interactions may not be well known at the time of requirements gathering. However, at an abstract level, the interactions are quite clear. As with transaction processing, documenting the actors for a use case for inquiry-only systems is very useful. You always need to know your audience!

2.4.2 Use Cases for Requests for Proposals

Requests for proposals (RFPs) are often used between a customer and a contractor. The customer issues an RFP to multiple contractors, the contractors bid to win the business by submitting proposals, and the customer picks a winner based on the compliance of the responses to the RFP.

RFPs can be tricky business for the customer and for the contractors. Especially with government work, the RFP for a computer system must be complete and unambiguous because the requirements that are itemized in it become the foundation for the creation of the system. Requirements lists are often used in RFPs, and because everyone is worried about legality and wants to avoid missing anything, these requirements lists can sometimes run hundreds of pages.

We suggest that you employ use cases for RFPs. If the customer were to create a set of use cases and scenarios in the RFP, the contractors could respond more easily and the solution would more likely reflect the business needs. Use cases can simplify RFPs and proposal responses in the same way that use cases simplify requirements for other types of systems requirements specifications.

2.4.3 Use Cases for Software Package Evaluation

Use cases have special applicability to software package evaluation efforts. Use cases can help clarify the "gap analysis" by comparing package functionality to business requirements. We have used this approach and have seen it used elsewhere with great success.

2.4.4 Use Cases for Non-Object-Oriented Systems

There is a predisposition in our industry to associate use cases with object-oriented systems. We believe that use cases can be used easily for non-object-oriented systems, and our experiences bear this out. Our use cases have been used to document requirements for a number of non-object-oriented systems.

The fact that use cases are part of the UML encourages the viewpoint that use cases are exclusively for object-oriented systems. However, we view use cases as a great way to document requirements for any system. In fact, we use them not only for system development efforts but also for evaluations and package implementation. Use cases are a good way to boil down the essential requirements of the required interactions, whether they are used for a new system being built or to help someone make a choice between packages that already exist.

2.5 Applying Use Cases to the Requirements Problem

We hope that you find this chapter a good primer to use cases. We love use cases, and we hope you've developed an appreciation for them as you've read through this chapter. We think they make a lot of sense as a tool for requirements, and, to this end, we've developed our own process for incorporating them into the requirements-gathering activity. Chapter 3 provides a view of our overall approach. Chapters 4 through 6, the methodology chapters, describe how to iterate through levels of fidelity with your use cases until you have everything you need to build a great system.

3

We never stop investigating. We are never satisfied that we know enough to get by. Every question we answer leads on to another question. This has become the greatest survival trick of our species.

—Desmond Morris

A Use-Case-Driven Approach to Requirements Gathering

3.1 Requirements Specification Tools

In Chapter 1, we reviewed how various techniques to gather requirements used today are not working. In Chapter 2, we examined the emergence of the Unified Modeling Language (UML) and use cases, and how those tools might be applied to the requirements problem.

In this chapter we propose a specific group of tools that help drive requirements gathering to a successful end product. In this context, *tools* does not refer to software applications; instead, tools are the techniques and methods that assist in requirements gathering and refining.

3.2 Principles for Requirements Success

We propose an approach to gathering and documenting requirements that differs substantially from what we have called the traditional approach. Our approach is *use-case-driven* and employs a number of tools that are either borrowed from the traditional approach, perhaps with slight changes, or are completely new. Chapters 1 and 2 discuss the current state of requirements gathering and the simple elegance of use cases. Now let's look at a solution to the requirements problem. Table 3.1 outlines several guiding principles and ways to succeed in fulfilling those principles.

Table 3.1   Guiding Principles

Guiding Principle	Comments
Reduce risk.	The obvious result of a high-risk project is a high failure rate caused by unhappy users and management. Culprits in increasing risk are big-bang requirements and micromanagement. Possible ways to reduce risk are an iterative or incremental approach, increased user involvement (users writing use cases), and requirements reviews.
Focus on business interactions.	Very often, technologists focus on technology and not on the business interactions required for a system. To focus the effort on the business, you must separate analysis and design activities and keep use cases devoid of technical language and considerations.
Reduce volume.	By turning requirements specification into requirements engineering (a term we've avoided), teams often produce huge amounts of requirements documentation. When they are asked to review it, users rebel, either by rubber-stamping everything (and complaining later) or by refusing to deal with it, causing schedule delays. Strategies for reducing volume are to leave the rote requirements (table maintenance and the like) until the end and to abstract use cases and business rules as much as possible.
Reduce duplicates and inconsistencies.	When a requirements specification exceeds 30 to 40 pages of text, confusion and sloppiness begin to creep in. The requirements become a poor basis from which the designers must work, and they give users a poor view of the system-to-be. The strategies for reducing duplicates and inconsistencies are the same as those used to reduce volume.
Create requirements that users can understand easily.	The main culprits of user-inappropriate requirements are premature design, overspecification, and insufficient user involvement or authoring. The main strategy for avoiding this issue is to employ use cases as specified in this book, avoiding implementation-specific language.

Guiding Principle	Comments
Create requirements that are useful to designers, developers, and project managers.	When requirements are useless, the main culprit is the requirements list: Failure to group, classify, cross-reference, or automate listed requirements hurts their usefulness. Also, if the requirements are not easily traceable to design artifacts, code, and test cases, they get no attention from designers, developers, and testers. By using use cases and a use-case-driven lifecycle, you can minimize or avoid these issues.
Leave a requirements trail.	Even with use cases and business rules, it is important to cross-reference the artifacts properly so that later traceability is possible. By taking a use-case-driven approach and creating real use cases from abstract use cases, the team can help leave a requirements trail that ensures a system built as it was specified (and promised!).
Leave design until later.	If requirements analysts are really designers-in-disguise, then design considerations can easily creep into requirements specifications.
Keep the plan in mind.	It is easy to get caught up in today's set of requirements tasks and forget what is to be done with these documents. It is the responsibility of the project manager to help the team keep a far-sighted perspective. Thinking about the use-case paths as increments of development helps the team in making decisions on the granularity of use cases.

3.3 Three Steps for Gathering Requirements

We suggest that requirements be created iteratively. Iterative and incremental approaches help reduce risk by treating risky items earlier in the lifecycle. Requirements specifications, as much or more than other lifecycle artifacts, change constantly and require frequent modifications and overhauls. This is because requirements are based on several people's fuzzy ideas about a computer application to be created. Other artifacts have the luxury of tying back to the requirements, but the requirements tie back only to fuzzy ideas.

Iterative creation of artifacts is highly dependent on individual situations. It would be silly to suggest that exactly the same number of iterations is needed to complete requirements in all situations. However, it is possible to say that iterative requirements specification always proceeds through the same logical steps in every situation. In this book we make a case for three logical steps: outlining, widening, and focusing. We have created names for each of these steps and have assigned those names to iterations. We do not want to specify that there always must be three iterations, only that there are three mind-sets to adopt throughout requirements. The iteration names are

- *Facade*—Outline and high-level descriptions
- *Filled*—Broadening and deepening
- *Focused*—Narrowing and pruning

Chapters 4 through 6 provide the details of these iterations.

The iterative and incremental lifecycle is not a set of lifecycle phases for requirements, something that would be cumbersome; rather, it is a way to categorize the activities needed to develop use cases. It is likely that most of the use cases will be in the same iteration at the same time, but we emphasize that it is not necessary to force use cases into iterations if it's not needed.

We created these named iterations because we've often been asked, "How many iterations are right?" "What should I do in each iteration?" It made sense to us to categorize requirements-gathering activities into a set of iterations, but please do not assume that we are asking you to approach these iterations rigidly as a set of lifecycle phases.

Throughout the iterations we create and refine several tools that define the requirements deliverable set. These tools include use cases (which require the most effort), and they provide comprehensive coverage of this part of the software development lifecycle.

- Mission, vision, values
- Statement of work
- Risk analysis
- Prototype
- Use cases and use case diagrams
- Business rule catalog

Let's take a look at each of these tools and its role in the requirements activity.

3.4 The Role of the Mission, Vision, Values

The *mission, vision, values (MVV)* of an application, probably the first document to be created, outlines the business problem to be solved. The authors of the MVV must be the high-level executives who are approving the need to solve the problem.

- *Mission*—What the project will "do"
- *Vision*—What the end product will "be"
- *Values*—What principles will guide the project while they do what they will do and build what will be

3.5 The Role of the Statement of Work

The *statement of work* defines the scope of the work and a general view of how the work is to be accomplished, including a general workplan and staffing assignments. The following is a sample outline of a statement of work, again from one of our previous engagements (with a little help from the RUP).

1. Scope
2. Objectives
3. Application overview
4. User demography
5. Constraints
6. Assumptions
7. Staffing and cost
8. Deliverable outlines
9. Expected duration

The statement of work becomes a contract between the IT group and the user department. It is also the tool that is used to define a contract between a consulting company and a customer.

3.6 The Role of the Risk Analysis

A risk analysis is a list of the risks that may influence the development of the application; the risks are prioritized by the impact of each risk if realized and the likelihood of the risk. The risk analysis helps establish clearly whether this development effort should even be attempted. Table 3.2 is an example of a risk analysis.

The *risk rating* is calculated by multiplying the days lost if it occurs and the likelihood it will happen. It represents the total days that should be reserved as a contingency to handle the possibility of this risk.

NOTE: This idea is from *Rapid Development* (McConnell 1996).

3.7 The Role of the Prototype

A prototype is a software mock-up of a system's user interface, but no more. It helps round out the requirements picture, showing the user interface requirements clearly and, often, interactively.

In our approach, we propose moving the prototype to a later stage in the lifecycle: after the requirements have had a chance to gel. Introducing user interfaces onscreen at this later stage is less of a distraction for the users and helps you to avoid the temptation to solve problems before they are understood. This problem is discussed further in Chapter 4.

Table 3.2 Sample Risk Analysis

No.	Category	Risk	Resolution Needed By	Status	Days Lost If It Occurs	Likelihood It Will Happen	Risk Rating
001	Interfaces	A new application needs to interface with SAP that has not yet been put into production. There could be schedule delays if this project must wait two months for the SAP project.	Jul 1, 2004	Unresolved	50	50%	25
002	User time	The majority of the user group is heavily involved in a reengineering effort. If the project team members cannot get their time, the project will be delayed.	May 15, 2004	Being investigated	70	80%	56

Technical prototyping is a design activity that reduces technological risk by letting the team try out the technically tough pieces of the solution before the design and build activities are properly under way. This is a great way to collapse assumptions, especially when the problems or toolkit involved is new. Prototyping performed simultaneously with requirements activities is not a part of the requirements process and is outside this book's scope.

3.8 The Roles of Use Cases

The major artifacts of this approach are use cases. The following few paragraphs describe the different roles played by use cases as tools of requirements specification.

3.8.1 Use Cases Are Effective Communication Vehicles

Use cases are the centerpiece of our approach to requirements gathering. The interactions they illustrate form the basis of most of the requirements that must be documented.

In our experience, use cases have the additional tremendous benefit of aiding effective communication between IT staff and users. Users seem to catch on to use cases better than almost any other document that IT people produce. Because use cases are boiled down to the essence of the desired interactions, users are not distracted by computer-specific jargon or nomenclature (DFDs, ERDs, class diagrams, and so forth) or by user interface details (graphical user interface [GU] mock-ups, user interface storyboards, prototypes, and so on). All that remains is the most basic information about the interactions between actor and application.

3.8.2 Use Cases Can Be Used for Functional and Nonfunctional Requirements

Use cases can portray functional and nonfunctional requirements effectively. Generally, functional requirements can be put into terms of interactions between an actor and the application. The exceptions can be specified as business rules. Nonfunctional requirements—such as performance, extensibility, and maintainability—can often be stated in terms of use case stereotypes. These stereotypes are added to the use case model after most of the functional requirements are incorporated.

The definitions of the stereotypes that handle nonfunctional requirements should be quite detailed and should be reviewed by users in the same way that use cases are reviewed.

3.8.3 Use Cases Help Ensure Requirements Traceability

Use cases can provide requirements traceability effectively through the lifecycle because they are a building block for system design, units of work, construction iterations, test cases, and delivery stages. The status of each use case, including how it has changed over time, becomes completely obvious to the users and the IT staff. If a new use case is added, it becomes evident that the scope has increased and therefore something about the project plan must change.

When use cases drive the lifecycle, it also helps to assure the stakeholders that all the requirements are being addressed as development progresses. For example, at any point in the lifecycle, anyone who is creating artifacts—whether they are design deliverables or code—should be able to answer this question: Which use case (or scenario) are you elaborating?

3.8.4 Use Cases Discourage Premature Design

Use cases discourage (although nothing can prevent) premature design. When design creeps into a use case, it becomes quite obvious. When the system is performing several steps before responding to a user, it sounds an alarm that perhaps internal system design is being created and exposed.

3.9 The Role of the Business Rules Catalog

Use cases are an important part of the requirements picture, but by themselves they are not enough. Use cases capture the interactions between users and the system, but they cannot portray all the subtleties of how a business is run. For this, we need *business rules*.

A list of business rules is not the same thing as a list of requirements. Business rules are the written and unwritten rules that dictate how a company or agency conducts its business. Requirements relate to a specific application being considered or developed.

In our methodology, we use a combination of use cases and business rules. Use cases cover a great many of the requirements by specifying interactions between actors and an application. However, these interactions are governed by the business rules that set the tone and environment in which the application operates. Some businesses create lists of business rules for their businesses even though they may not be building any new computer applications. It is simply important to them to document how their business runs.

According to Ellen Gottesdiener (2002) author and consultant, there are five categories of business rules:

- *Structural facts*—Facts or conditions that must be true. Example: The first customer contact is always with a salesperson.
- *Action restricting*—Prohibiting one or more actions based on a condition. Example: Do not accept a check from a customer who does not have an acceptable credit history.
- *Action triggering*—Instigating an action when one or more conditions become true. Example: Send the shipment as soon as the pick items (items selected from inventory) have been collected.
- *Inferences*—Drawing a conclusion when one or more conditions become true. Example: Members who fly more than 100,000 miles in one calendar year become Elite members.
- *Calculations*—Calculating one value given a set of other values. Example: The sales amount is the total retail value of the line items but does not include state or federal tax.

Business rules must be *atomic*: Each business rule should be stated at the finest level of granularity possible. Methods of atomizing tend to be more art than science.

The best way to get a feel for business rules is to see lots of examples (see Table 3.3). We've provided some examples from our experiences and our imagination and have categorized them in several ways:

- Type of rule
- Likelihood of change (whether the rule is static or dynamic)
- Source

Your business rules catalog may look significantly different, depending on the type of data you record and cross-reference.

NOTE: It is easy to slip into the trap of creating a list of business rules that is actually a list of requirements. Remember that business rules always relate to how a company operates; they do not relate to the requirements of a specific application. A requirement is usually phrased, "The system shall," whereas a business rule states, "The business works like this."

Table 3.3 We-Rent-All Equipment Rentals Co. Business Rules Catalog Sample

No.	Rule Definition	Type of Rule	Static/ Dynamic	Source
001	Cash, personal check, and credit card are accepted for rental payment.	Action restricting	Dynamic	Management policy
002	Customers who rent driving equipment must possess a U.S. driver's license.	Action restricting	Static	Management policy
003	Customers who rent driving equipment must provide proof of insurance for the rental.	Action restricting	Static	Management policy
004	Rentals must be returned by the next day at the same time as the conclusion of the rental transaction, unless otherwise specified at the time of rental or in a requested extension.	Action restricting	Static	Management policy

continues

Table 3.3 *continued*

No.	Rule Definition	Type of Rule	Static/ Dynamic	Source
005	If a rental item is not available, substitute using the substitution part chart.	Action triggering	Static	Management policy
006	Customers can make reservations up to six months in advance.	Action restricting	Dynamic; advance limit may change	Management policy
007	Rental items will be serviced according to the part service chart.	Action triggering	Static	Management policy
008	If a rental item that was reserved is not available to the customer on the day of the rental for any reason, the customer service representative will arrange for the customer to rent it from a competitor at our cost.	Action triggering	Dynamic; customer service level may change	Management policy
009	If customers are renting firearms, a background check must be initiated and a 30-day waiting period is required.	Action triggering	Dynamic; law may change	Federal law
010	A customer may return an item only if it has not yet been taken out of the store.	Structural facts	Static	Management policy

3.10 Managing Success

Adopting a use-case-driven approach can help you organize and systematize your software development efforts. This chapter describes a series of steps you can take to produce a set of documents that will help you carefully define your system's requirements. The next three chapters discuss the three iterations that we recommend, explaining how the use cases we've introduced are used to drive and guide the process overall.

4

The Facade Iteration

4.1 Objectives

The first iteration in the requirements lifecycle is the Facade iteration. Its purpose is to create placeholders for each major interaction you expect the actors to have with the application.

A Facade use case contains only the minimum information needed as a placeholder, including a name and short description of the interaction. It also identifies the initiating actor and other actors. Executing this iteration is difficult because you may not yet have a

The Facade Iteration

concept of the application. For this reason, the team will do its best work if the environment encourages openness and creativity.

As you develop a definition of the proposed system, you can call on the following sources for ideas and opinions:

- Users
- Project team
- Industry experts
- IT management
- User management
- Owners of the data

4.1.1 Users

The users have the major influence on the definition of proposed system interactions. They are the focus of the new system, and their input and buy-in are critical.

However, as anyone knows who has been through requirements definition even once, the users cannot tell you the whole story. They are not equipped to define fully what the new system should do. Why? First, the new system is probably not being created merely to automate an existing system. Many new business processes, perhaps not yet built, will dictate the system interactions. In addition, the users often know their domain so well that they assume that most of what they do is terribly obvious. Alternatively, they've been put into their current role recently as a result of organizational restructuring, and they haven't had time to become familiar with their environment. One department in an oil and gas company for which we worked had a 110 percent annual staff attrition rate, so relying solely on the users was not possible for that development effort. In any case, the requirements-gathering team has its work cut out for it.

There's another issue. If you don't have a *subject matter expert* (SME) on your project team who knows this domain as well as a user, your team will not have the opportunity to "read between the lines" of what the users tell you. You need to make these kinds of inferences to identify better, faster, cheaper processes and to recognize the vital pieces of the puzzle that the users have left out—omissions that will come back to bite you in three months' time. SMEs are often ex-users themselves, or they may be IT people who have specialized in an industry and have a number of system implementations under their belts.

4.1.2 Project Team

The project team, too, has input into how the user-system interactions should occur. After all, the team is responsible for the work! The project team should have a focus on setting standards for interaction, maintaining scope, making inferences from user input, and documenting, storing, and indexing the requirements. The major guiding force behind these interactions should be the users and the SMEs on your project team. The task of the rest of the team is to transmute these models into use cases. The users provide the information on how they do things now and what they would like to see changed, and the SMEs help to shape the system into more refined, elegant, and profitable processes.

4.1.3 Industry Experts

The challenge of the project team members is to take *user-centric* information offered by computer industry experts and luminaries and to determine whether it applies to this situation. Industry experts can provide only rules of thumb, and rules are meant to be broken. Determine your position on the industry "advice-of-the-day," and if you decide to deviate from it be prepared to defend your position. Whatever you do, don't simply follow the experts blindly. Unless you believe in your direction, your project won't work.

4.1.4 IT Management Group

The IT management group always has opinions on how the interactions of the system should be described. If you are a member of the in-house IT group, you must balance these opinions with the user needs and wants. If you are an outside consultant the same balancing act is required, but sometimes it is easier being a third party. The IT group can provide valuable input regarding systems that have been developed previously, interfaces between user departments, previous incarnations of this functionality, and other contextual information.

As with user input, you should be cautious in weighing IT viewpoints. IT staff (yes, this means us!) have a strong tendency to push requirements gathering into something that is technology-centered. Technology-centric solutions have no place in this early activity of system development. It is dangerous to commit an application to a specific technology or

*Requirements analysts need to wear blinders to avoid
thinking about the various technology options.*

User-Centric Versus Technology-Centric Solutions

User-centric solutions focus on what the user needs. All requirements that drive the development of use cases come from actual business needs of the users. This principle applies to the entire development cycle and not just requirements gathering.

Technology-centric solutions focus on using the "technology of the hour" for whatever business problem might pop up. Applying a technical solution—whether a new programming language, operating system, architecture, partitioning scheme, or methodology—becomes an end in itself rather than a tool. It is sometimes a fine distinction, but it is possible to tell the difference.

We're not saying you shouldn't try out new technology to solve business problems, but when you find yourself adding features the user didn't request simply because your new tool supports them, you've crossed the line into a technology-centric approach. By the same token, when you are trying to convince the users that they should not want a feature because your favorite tool doesn't support it, you are being technology-centric. When you start making up business problems so that you can use your new techno-toy, you are also being technology-centric.

Our best advice: Start user-centric and never lose that focus. The time to start deciding how to "make it happen" is during design. If there are critical requirements that can't be fulfilled, decide then to take them out.

to focus more on the technical implementation than the needs of the users. This practice leads to systems that fit neatly into technology niches but are lacking in functionality or may even deliver functions that are not required. It's easy to fall into the technology trap, especially for someone who is steeped in technical know-how. At this stage, there should be no discussion of technical solutions, only a focus on business solutions. Technical solutions enter into the picture during systems analysis and design, which are the next activities of the lifecycle.

4.1.5 User Management Personnel

User management personnel are involved in the major decisions for the application's life or death, so it is important to try to involve them early and often. They need to know of major changes in the project's scope and should be kept up-to-date on major decisions that are made throughout the life of the project—for example, whether to use distributed updates or centralized updates.

4.1.6 Owners of the Data

The users of the proposed application may not be the owners of the data—that is, the people who are responsible for the integrity of the data in the database. From a technical standpoint, of course, the database administrators are responsible for data integrity. But from a user perspective, there may be an administrative group, such as an audit or finance group, that is responsible for seeing that the data is accurate and current. Whoever they are, they will also want input into the requirements and should be involved as much as possible.

4.2 Steps in the Facade Iteration

Following are the steps to completing the Facade iteration:

1. Create a problem statement.
2. Identify and review existing documentation and intellectual capital.
3. Get the executive sponsor's unique viewpoint.
4. Review business process definitions.
5. Identify the users, the user group management, the stakeholders, the customers being served by the user group, and the owners of the data.
6. Interview the stakeholders.
7. Create a stakeholders' list.
8. Find the actors.
9. Create the use case survey (a list of Facade use cases).
10. Start the nonfunctional requirements survey.
11. Start the business rules catalog.
12. Create a risk analysis.
13. Create a statement of work.
14. Begin experimenting with user interface metaphors.
15. Begin user interface storyboards.
16. Get informal approval from the executive sponsor.

4.2.1 Create the Mission, Vision, Values

The executive sponsor leads the effort to create the mission, vision, and values for the application and distributes it widely to generate support and awareness. This document essentially becomes the marching orders for the application development team, including the requirements analysts. For an example of mission, vision, and values, refer to Chapter 3.

4.2.2 Identify and Review Existing Documentation and Intellectual Capital

To familiarize yourself with the history of this effort, read every memo, deliverable, proposal, and e-mail message you can get your hands on. If there is too much for one person to read, use a team approach. Each person takes a stack of paper or electronic documents and wades through it, reporting the interesting findings to the group. Here are the questions you're trying to answer:

- What elements of the proposed system were ruled out previously and by whom? Who introduced those items in the first place?
- Who are the people who want this system built? Who doesn't want it built?
- Have any commercial off-the-shelf (COTS) packages been considered? Which ones?
- Is this project visible to upper management? Who?
- How long has this idea been kicked around? What were its previous incarnations?

The benefit of completing this step is that you create a *reuse strategy* at the first level: requirements. If someone has already done part of this work, it is worthwhile to try reusing it. Of course, reuse always comes with some overhead, so you must judge whether it is worth it. Often, it is. Major stumbling blocks are revealed, and fortuitous shortcuts will become clear.

Let's take a closer look at each of these questions.

4.2.2.1 What Elements of the Proposed System Were Ruled Out Previously and by Whom?

You're not searching for great detail here, only the subsystem name and general functionality that was killed before this effort started. Usually there is a long "fuzzy front end" (McConnell 1996) during which not much gets done but people mull the possibility of developing such a system. What was ruled out during this time?

4.2.2.2 Who Are the People Who Want This System Built? Who Doesn't Want It Built?

This question may be more important than the first one. Find out the enemies of this system and their motivations. If possible, arrange to meet with them, or at least people in the organization who know something about them. At this point, don't try to convince them that they're wrong. Just gather data. They may have valid suggestions, and implementing them might result in only a small change to the requirements that would be easy to include at this early point. The motives of these naysayers may be political, and it will require your tact, charm, and negotiation skills to work with them. If you're a consultant or a low-ranking IT team member, this is a difficult step because the upper-level IT managers may not understand why this kind of discussion is important. However, you should still see how far you can go. Consider it practice in office politics for when you're in management. Remember that numerous systems have died for political and not technical reasons.

4.2.2.3 Have Any Packages Been Considered? Which Ones?

It is important to ferret out this information. There may have been some investigation into whether any COTS packages could fulfill the requirements for this system. It is also likely that those COTS packages have evolved since the investigation. Check into it. During design, you can evaluate the suitability of these products.

4.2.2.4 This Project Visible to Upper Management? Who?

High project visibility is both a curse and a gift. The curse is often that everyone wants his or her trademark on the visible project and wants to be associated with it—until it begins to look as if there are problems. However, project visibility is a greater gift than a curse. When resources are required, it helps tremendously because no one wants to stand in the way of an initiative that has support and visibility at high levels of management. Quite simply, the higher the visibility in the organization, the better.

4.2.2.5 How Long Has This Idea Been Kicked Around? What Were Its Previous Incarnations?

Find out what you can in this area, but don't go into great detail. Because elements of these previous incarnations will show up in your requirements, it pays to at least speak the language: "Oh, that sounds like it comes from the ORMS idea a few years ago." It's likely that this system has been attempted once or twice before and then stopped.

> **Too Much Information**
>
> Following this process, the team will inevitably complain that there is too much information to cope with intelligently. Our advice is that the team allows this to happen and tries to find a way to deal with the overabundance of information. It is quite likely that a small team of business analysts will not be able to read through all the background documents. However, humans are incredibly adaptive to challenges like this and our brains are able to quickly sort the wheat from the chaff until "enough" of the primary messages are clear.

4.2.3 Get the Executive Sponsor's Unique Viewpoint

It can be hard to get time from your executive sponsor. She is rushing from one high-flying meeting to another, and she has already started organizing her next big launch. As far as she's concerned, you should be self-sufficient. Yet your success rides on getting the exact definition of the problem from her. Get at least a sliver of her time, whatever it takes. Try this as your opening line: "Our team has our own answers to these questions, but we want to make sure we're right." Then ask her these questions.

- What is the problem being solved?
- Why is a system required?
- Why is a computer system required?
- Who will be affected by the system implementation? How?

There is another very important question to ask the executive sponsor. "How can we make sure this application helps fulfill our corporate mission, vision, and values?" The application your team is building must have "traceability" back to the goals of the business as a whole. This is true whether your organization is a private or public corporation, non-profit or government department. The organization is tasked with accomplishing some goal, and each and every task under the umbrella of the organization must be aligned with that goal. Make sure you ask the sponsor, or whoever else can help with the answer.

These questions are best addressed in a face-to-face meeting or telephone call. E-mail will not work. This must be interactive. Certain things the sponsor says will spur other questions, and you should ask them. It is important to try to catch every nuance, every uncomfortable moment, every glance at her shoes. Body language, silences, and tone of voice will warn you of the dangers to come. Remember, if she's not happy with the result, you've failed. Period.

4.2.3.1 What Is the Problem Being Solved?

This should be a problem statement, perhaps four or five sentences at the most. It should describe the business reason for the system. Usually, business systems are developed to help the organization stay competitive in the marketplace, to provide better customer service, to automate certain functions, to comply with government legislation, or to meet any other of a variety of environmental demands. State the factor that is pushing the need for this system, and state what is likely to occur if it is not developed. If there is a drop-dead date that has relevance to the problem statement, include it.

4.2.3.2 Why Is a System Required?

What is the worst thing that would happen if this problem were not resolved? How much money would the new process save (or make) the company? What is a reasonable payback time? This question addresses only the business process and not necessarily a computer system. That's next.

4.2.3.3 Why Is a Computer System Required?

Why can't this task be done manually? If the business process has been proven, why can't it be a manual process? This is a difficult question. If the executive sponsor starts to think about it, she may decide that an electronic system isn't needed at all, and that means you will have to find another project to work on! As project managers, we tend to jump too quickly into a self-fulfilling prophecy: We want to make a project happen whether or not it is *meant* to happen. If you take a hard, objective look at whether this system really should be built now, you might save countless heartaches later.

If you and the executive sponsor end up talking each other out of a computer system to attack this problem, the executive sponsor may see you as someone who has just saved her budget millions of dollars, and she may be more likely to come to you again with requests, knowing that you'll take an objective view. Play the devil's advocate with the sponsor. Pretend that you need to be convinced of the need for this process to be automated. It's what's best for the business.

4.2.3.4 Who Will Be Affected by the System Implementation? How?

Identify all the groups that will be affected by this implementation. Determine the relative benefits or obstacles they will experience from this system. Judge this over a period of time. For example, the data entry clerks might be disadvantaged by the system at first but then realize its benefits after two months. This technique is called *other people's views*, or OPV (de Bono 1994). Don't limit the list to those directly affected; include the indirect effects as well. This step will give you valuable information later as you calculate costs versus benefits.

Other People's Views: The Selling Property Application

At the beginning of a project to design a real estate application, the following people and groups were identified as those who would be affected by the application.

All stakeholders want a system that is easy to use, doesn't cost much, handles transactions quickly, and stays out of the way, allowing productivity.

Buyers want to buy a property that fits their exact needs and want some advice on shaping their own needs.

Sellers want to sell property quickly and as close to their target price as possible.

Agents want to earn maximum fees in minimal time and want to feel a sense of accomplishment from helping people exchange money and property.

The owner of the agency wants the application to increase the agency's profits, wants the application to be delivered quickly, and wants control of and information about the status of the development.

Regulatory agencies, although they have no financial stake in the system, have power over the results. Think about the government tax agencies, industry regulators, stock exchange regulators, and so on.

Designers and developers want requirements that show the needs of the users accurately, want no design assumptions embedded in requirements, and want to build an application that is state-of-the-art.

4.2.4 Review the Business Process Definitions

If there is business process documentation relevant to the application you are building, review it before you proceed. Business processes can be documented as flowcharts, activity diagrams, or even use cases.

We discuss the traceability between the business process definitions and the system use cases in Chapter 7.

4.2.5 Identify the Users, Customers, and Related Groups

Get an up-to-date organization chart for the user group that includes management and all participants. Try to find out where the informal power lies. If you can also get last year's organization chart, so much the better. Seeing the way things have been reorganized will help you understand where the organization is trying to go and how a system could help it get there.

If possible, talk to a sampling of the users. Take some of them out for lunch. Include not only the managers but also a decent sampling across the board. These are get-to-know-you sessions and not requirements gathering—yet. That comes later.

By *customers*, we mean the real, honest-to-goodness customers outside the organization, not internal customers. Building a system for a grocery chain? Identify the people who would benefit: the clerks, the shoppers, the pharmacists. How about a manufacturing firm? Identify the wholesalers and the final customers, assuming that your system will change how they view the firm.

The "Internal Customer" Problem

A recent movement promotes the idea of treating everyone in the organization as your customer. The IT shop treats the accountants as its customers, the accountants treat manufacturing as their customer, and so forth. Here's the issue with internal customers. Let's say you work for an internal IT shop that's building a sales tracking system, and you consider your internal customer to be the sales department. Your internal customers will tell you exactly what they want so that they can sell more stuff, properly credit their commissions, and widen their markets. That's part of why you're building this system. But there's more. The *actual* customers will want a sales tracking system that increases their level of customer service, allows them to cancel orders late in the order process, and is flexible enough to handle their specialized requests. They may also offer some insights into what the future may hold for this company in terms of the changing marketplace. Christopher Alexander, an insightful building architect who has greatly influenced the computer industry, said at the 1996 OOPSLA conference in San Jose that computer analysts and programmers treat themselves as "guns for hire" in their organizations. They say, "Just tell us what to build, and we'll build it"—without asking about the larger circumstances. By including the external customers in the process of requirements gathering, we broaden our purview to include the health and wealth of the entire business, and perhaps society, in the development of an application. We believe that it is the obligation of computer analysts and programmers everywhere to delve deeply to determine the true requirements of the systems they build.

4.2.6 Interview the Stakeholders

You can do this task in several ways. You can conduct individual interviews with the users, user management, and a sampling of their customers. You can hold a concentrated joint requirements planning session, during which all interested parties get together in a hotel conference room and work through all the issues until a semblance of requirements emerges. The differences in these approaches change the speed, but not the content, of your iterations. You will most likely emerge from the JRP with a set of Filled use cases, which will need to be consolidated with the Focused iterations before they are completely usable. This means that to avoid wasting the participants' time you may need to walk into the JRP with a set of Facade use cases. With individual interviews, on the other hand, the interview notes will come together as input to your Facade use cases. Remember Ellen Gottesdiener's book on requirements workshops as a useful tool (Gottesdiener 2002).

4.2.7 Create a Stakeholders List

Once you've identified the stakeholders and had some discussion with them, create a simple list of them. Stakeholders will come from inside the organization you're providing a solution for. They will also come from outside that organization. Outside stakeholders may include customers, suppliers, partner companies, resellers, investors, and people in other departments (if it's a departmental application). Remember, a stakeholder is someone who has a direct "stake" in the success of the system. A rule of thumb to use is to think about whether someone in this category would be willing to spend a week of their time (given reasonable notice) to make sure this application goes well. If yes, they are a potential stakeholder.

4.2.8 Find the Actors

Actors are the people and applications that interact with this application. Ask the executive sponsor who she thinks the actors are, and ask each stakeholder.

Your definition of the actors may be fuzzy at this point, and that is OK. Define them as they arise and push concerns about duplication and definition into later iterations. At this point, consider every stakeholder as a potential actor.

4.2.9 Create the Use Case Survey (A List of Facade Use Cases)

The output of this step is a list of sketchy use cases that outlines the scope of the proposed system. The level of detail is crucial because too much detail here will hurt the iterative nature of this process. It is important to identify the need for the use case, describe in two or three sentences what is involved, and move on.

We're creating use cases that treat the system as if it were a bread-making machine. You put the ingredients into the machine, and after a while you take out a loaf of bread. The focus is on the ingredients going in and the product coming out. What goes on inside the bread-making machine is not our concern, and certainly not part of requirements.

Facade use cases show the basic, essential, high-level interactions that this application must support (Constantine 1999).

Use cases focus on the ingredients that go in and the result that comes out.

When you're creating use cases, do

- Name the use case in user terminology.
- Write a two- or three-sentence description of what the use case accomplishes.
- Use role names and not user titles.
- Group input or output information without specifying field-by-field details, which can come in later iterations.

Don't

- Skip use cases, because the goal is to create "shell" use cases for each of the main user interactions expected for this system (placeholders, remember?).
- Start with CRUD (create-read-update-delete) table-based use cases (leave them until you have identified use cases that satisfy business requirements).

Table 4.1 shows a use case survey. Consider each line on this survey a Facade use case.

Actor names and use case names can be quite informal and may not be completely consistent in Facade. They can be cleaned up later.

4.2.10 Collect and Document Nonfunctional Requirements

There are three steps to identifying and documenting nonfunctional requirements in this iteration:

1. Identify the requirement in the notes from previous interviews.
2. Validate the requirement with additional interviews with the associated stakeholders.
3. Document the requirement: Capture an understanding of the requirement, its effects, and the system and business degradation that would result if the requirement were not satisfied.

Table 4.1 Use Case Survey

Use Case Number
Use Case Name
Initiating Actor
Description
Completeness
Maturity
Use Case Complexity
Architectural Priority
Business Priority
Dependency
Source
Comments

In the Filled and Focused iterations, you refine your nonfunctional requirements and create a stereotype to relate nonfunctional requirements to the use cases. Stereotypes are first explored in Chapter 2, in which we describe how this feature of the UML can be employed to associate related information to a number of use cases. For this iteration, we only capture and document these requirements.

4.2.10.1 Identify Nonfunctional Requirements

The best time to identify nonfunctional requirements (see Table 4.2) is while you are exploring the functional requirements. Whenever you identify a candidate nonfunctional requirement, document it. Do not wait to attempt to do this as a single task later. Your group of users is an excellent source for identifying nonfunctional requirements. When you interview stakeholders while building the use cases, use this opportunity to gather the nonfunctional requirements, too.

Ask the users about response time needs, and ask them what annoys them about the way the system works now. The answers will give you valuable leads for nonfunctional requirements. If there is a legacy system, it can be another good source for nonfunctional requirements. Ask users what they liked and disliked about it. Be careful not to confuse business-related gripes with those that provide nonfunctional requirements. For example, "The existing system only allows us to capture three lines of miscellaneous information about a customer." Increasing this length constraint can be documented as a normal requirement. The flow of events would contain the statement "Enter the miscellaneous information provided by the customer (no length constraint)."

Table 4.2 Definitions of Nonfunctional Requirements

Nonfunctional Requirement	Definition
Archival	Length of time data needs to be retained within the application; level of difficulty to retrieve archived data (special request to operator, and so on)
Auditability	Ability for this application to show what has happened to it, who did it, and when (audit trail, transaction changes, before/after pictures, and so on); includes requirements for effective dating
Authentication	Security requirement to ensure "you are who you say you are"
Authorization	Security requirement to ensure that users can access only certain functions within the application (by use case, subsystem, Web page, business rule, field-level, and so on)
Availability	24×7 support and 99.999% uptime or better (this would be a very aggressive availability requirement)
Compatibility	Adherence to industry standards for inputs/outputs (XML, ebXML, BPML, and so on)
Configurability	Ability for the end users to change aspects of the software's configuration easily (through usable user interfaces)
Data integrity	Tolerance for loss, corruption, or duplication of data
Extensibility	Ability to easily incorporate add-on modules (components) of functionality to the application in production
Installability	Ease of system installation on all necessary platforms
Integratability	Ability for this application to easily fit in as part of a larger system (for example, ERP component and others)
Interoperability	APIs (application programming interfaces) required to allow other applications to talk to our application easily. This is unique from *compatibility* because interoperability is concerned only with the structure and ease of use of the APIs, not the industry standard protocols.
Leverageability/ reuse	Ability to leverage common components across multiple products
Localization	Support for multiple languages (German, Chinese, and so on) on entry/query screens, in data fields; on reports; multi-byte character requirements (such as Kanji and others); also units-of-measure; currencies

Nonfunctional Requirement	Definition
Maintainability	Amount of effort required to maintain (and enhance) application in production
Multiple environment support	Need to run multiple environments on a single server (development, system test, user test, and so on)—this could mean that the application components can never "hold and lock" vital operating system ports or resources, like a CD-ROM drive or port 8080 to the Internet
Operability	Ease of everyday operation; amount of qualification and training required for operators to oversee and troubleshoot the application
Performance	Constraints in batch (overnight window) and online
Personalization	Ability for individual users to personalize their view of the application (My Yahoo! Style)
Portability	Ability to easily move the application to different hardware platforms, operating systems, database management systems, network protocols, etc.
Privacy	Ability to hide transactions from internal company employees (transactions encrypted so even database administrators [DBAs] and network architects cannot see them)
Reliability	Confidence in the accuracy of transactions processed in the application
Robustness	Ability to handle error and boundary conditions while running (internet connection goes down, power outage, hardware failure/replacement, and so on)
Scalability	Ability to handle a wide variety of system configuration sizes and requirements
Security	General security requirements (encryption levels over the Internet, hackerproofing, viruses, and so on)
Upgradeability	Ability to easily/quickly upgrade from a previous version of this application to a newer version on servers and clients (upgrade scripts versus manual upgrades)
Usability/ achievability	Level of training required for users to achieve their goals with the application. Usability requirements need to be treated as seriously as any other architectural issue (performance, availability, and so on). Many applications fail because they are hard to use and nonintuitive.

These nonfunctional requirements, and many others like them, contribute to the usefulness of a system. For a number of reasons, however, it is common for these topics never to come up during requirements discussions. They are important nevertheless.

TIP: One way to deal with nonfunctional requirements is to rate their relative importance, numbering them 1 through *n*.

When confronted with a list of nonfunctional requirements, businesspeople always have the same response: "We'd like them all high priority, thanks!" Even businesspeople who understand that use cases must be prioritized and delivered in stages seem to think that computer applications are magically able to fulfill every nonfunctional requirement without any additional work. As you probably know, just the opposite is true. Nonfunctional requirements, contributing to architectural requirements, often cost more than the implementation of the use cases! A strict performance requirement of, say subsecond response time for 10,000 concurrent users could require such massive architecture that the cost would dwarf what was required to build a few Java programs to implement the use cases.

When businesspeople think about availability, for instance, they assume that having the application up "all the time" is no problem. Essentially, they initially are assuming "infinite availability." Our response when businesspeople make this assumption is to mention that *infinite availability will cost an infinite amount.* Usually, that is not the price they had in mind. This goes for every nonfunctional requirement. Businesspeople are adept negotiators, once they can understand some general cost parameters around each nonfunctional requirement level, they are happy to trade up and down until there is a solution they can live with. Don't let their initial assumptions drive you into an architectural nightmare.

It is quite likely that there will be multiple nonfunctional requirements in each category. Number the individual nonfunctionals and use the categories merely to add information to the entries.

4.2.10.2 Validate the Requirements

At this point, it helps to recap the functional and nonfunctional requirements and walk through them to test whether they make sense as a group.

4.2.10.3 Document Nonfunctional Requirements

Figure 4.1 presents a template for documenting the nonfunctional requirements.

Describe the requirement, include the exceptions that are special cases of the requirement, and name the use cases that it applies to. Some nonfunctional requirements, overall system constraints, apply to many use cases. It is not necessary to list all of them; instead, write, "Most data entry use cases." This approach spares you from having to write the same requirement for many use cases and makes it easier to alter. You can be more specific later.

Be careful to avoid including assumptions in the nonfunctional requirements. For example, a technical requirement might be expressed as "Back up nightly to tape storage."

Nonfunctional Category	Number	NFR Name	Description	Completeness	Maturity	Source	Comments	Outstanding Issues

Figure 4.1 *Technical Requirements Template*

Table 4.3 *Manage Property* Nonfunctional Requirements

Requirement	Exceptions	Applies to Use Cases
When an offer is changed, this information must be available to all users simultaneously.	None	Making and responding to offers
Other users, and anyone outside the system, must not be able to see details of any transactions being posted.	Authorized system administrators may view the details of any transaction.	All

The requirement is to prevent data loss, and it describes the frequency of this task. The mention of a tape solution, however, is either an architectural assumption or a technical constraint. Ask the user which it is. If it is a technical constraint, you have identified an additional nonfunctional requirement. If it is not, you risk adding an invalid assumption to your requirements.

Avoid documenting platitudes such as "Each window must have a method of closing it as part of the interface." Such statements do not add value to your use cases, but they may be appropriate rules in the user interface standards document.

Table 4.3 lists nonfunctional requirements for one use case example.

Nonfunctional Versus System Maintenance Requirements

Are system maintenance requirements different from nonfunctional requirements?

Yes. If you can model a requirement by writing a narrative description of the interaction between actor and system, then it is a functional requirement. Use cases can document any functional requirement, whether it involves maintaining a system or supporting a business process. Therefore, you should not document administrative functions as part of the nonfunctional requirements. A system administrator is another actor, and use cases are an appropriate vehicle to document the administrator's interactions. Write these use cases just as you would any other.

For example, many data-intensive applications use lookup tables to constrain the data. The requirement that the system administrator needs access and can change these tables is a functional requirement. This requirement could be documented in a use case titled *Edit List of States* with the actor *system administrator*.

Remember to investigate and document maintenance requirements. Because they are not core to the business, they are sometimes neglected.

TIP: When you're looking for nonfunctional requirements, refer to standards documents, where some technical constraints and requirements have probably been documented. Many organizations create and maintain standards documents to describe solutions to recurring problems. They can include everything from GUI standards to the software and hardware that is normally used. You should review these documents and become familiar with their contents. When you discover an already defined nonfunctional requirement, simply determine that it relates to your use case and state that it follows the established standard. This fits our principle of documenting only in one place whenever possible.

4.2.11 Start the Business Rules Catalog

Business rules (see Chapter 3) govern how the organization conducts its business, so they likely apply to several or all use cases.

Look for business rules that constrain the construction of use cases for this application. Try to produce at least a few rules in this early iteration, but there is no need to create a comprehensive catalog yet. See Table 4.4 for an example.

4.2.12 Create a Risk Analysis

Create a risk analysis document in this iteration as a repository for the risks that surface as you proceed through discussions with the users. Chapter 3 describes the format and role of the risk analysis.

4.2.13 Create a Statement of Work

Create a statement of work as a contract to fulfill during this development effort. This document outlines a set of scope boundaries that you and the user groups agree to. Chapter 3 describes the format and role of the statement of work.

4.2.14 Begin Experimenting with User Interface Metaphors

Early in the Facade iteration is the time to begin trying different user interface metaphors for applications that have a substantial amount of human interface. A metaphor is something that the user interface will represent, some tangible organizing mechanism. Some examples of metaphors:

- A neighborhood (Talk City, Geocities)
- A retail store (Amazon.com, Outpost)
- An auction house (eBay)
- A conference room or stadium (eRoom, WebEx)
- A personal calendar and address book (Palm Pilot, Pocket PC)

Table 4.4 Business Rules Example

Rule ID	Name	Description	Category	Static/ Dynamic	Source
001	Provide discounts for referrals.	If a current customer provides a referral to the company and the referral makes a purchase, the person referring the business receives a $20 discount off future costume purchases.	Inference	Dynamic	Interview with owner 5/7/2000
002	Referral discounts must be used quickly.	If a referral discount has been granted to a customer, that discount must be used on a costume within 1 year unless the customer contacts the company to request an extension.	Structural fact	Dynamic	Interview with owner 5/7/2000

Metaphors help the users to intuitively move around the functions without having to be trained keystroke-by-keystroke to know where to go. If you have the name of a new contact you've made, you know that you should go to the place marked "Address Book" and then look for something that says "Add" or "New."

However, metaphors can fall apart too. Here's how Alan Cooper (1995), a user interface guru, describes the failed General Magic MagiCap user interface in his book *About Face: The Essentials of User Interface Design*:

> I'm sure it was a lot of fun to design. I'll bet it is a real pain to use. Once you have learned that the substantial-looking building with the big AT&T on its façade is the phone company, you must forever live with going in and out of that building to call people. This most-modern, information-age software drags all the limitations of the mechanical age into the future and forces us to live with them yet again. Is this progress? (page 62)

Interface design is best left to the experts. Hire or contract with a "usabililty analyst" who has knowledge of how to craft user interfaces in a way that is intuitive for people. A lot of people talk about "usability studies" instead of "usability design." A usability study implies that someone will come in after the fact and examine what the technical designers have done, critique it, and be on their way. To us, this seems backwards. Good usability design from the start can create huge savings in user training and can also be the "make or break" between the application being accepted by its users or not. Yes, usability costs money, but if you can find the right usability person (or team) you will receive a very high return-on-investment.

4.2.15 Begin User Interface Storyboards

User interface design usually means creation of storyboards. Storyboards, borrowed from the television advertising world, are large cardboard wall charts with smaller pictures pasted on depicting each "scene." In a television ad, the storyboard may have one scene of the person waking up with the cough, one scene where the spouse is offering his comments, another where the magic cough remedy is consumed, and a last scene where everyone is sleeping happily.

The same pattern applies to user interface (UI) storyboards, which show how a user may navigate through the Web pages or screens to accomplish a goal. These UI storyboards will match the definitions of use case paths, but since the use cases aren't much more than names and descriptions at this point, the storyboards are still just graphic depictions of data entry, reporting, and other functions. It still makes sense to begin the storyboarding effort in the Facade iteration, since there will be a lot of discussion about colors, metaphors, and field placement yet to come.

Again, this is work for a professional. There are specialists who create Web sites and applications, usually called graphic designers or user interface specialists. Make sure that the people you use for this task have some basic knowledge of usability, or there will be problems between the usability analyst and the graphic designer.

4.2.16 Get Informal Approval from the Executive Sponsor

It is doubtful that you'll get your executive sponsor's attention long enough to leaf through a set of partially finished (Facade) use cases at this point. Instead, summarize what you believe are the sticking points: areas that are unclear, fraught with danger, or contentious. Bring these up with your sponsor and create an action item for each one as necessary. This is really all you need to do for this step.

4.3 Tools

4.3.1 The Use Case Diagram

In the Facade iteration, create a use case diagram for each Facade use case. Whether you put multiple use cases on one diagram in your diagramming tool is up to you—it doesn't matter. At this point, you will only be able to show the initiating actor as a stick figure and the use case bubble with its name. It may seem trivial, but it is worthwhile to begin now so there is a basis once the details start arriving from the next iteration.

Figure 4.2 shows an example of a use case diagram in the Facade iteration.

4.3.2 The Hierarchy Killer

Hierarchies of requirements must die. With use cases, we have the chance to abandon this aged technique in favor of a better approach. Remember that functional decomposition has a host of issues that complicate requirements specification (see Chapter 2). Yet, with use cases, we all have a strong tendency to put use cases into neat hierarchies that look shockingly

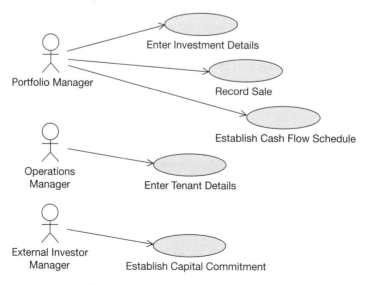

Figure 4.2   *Use Case Diagram Sample*

like functional decomposition. Some approaches even color-code the levels in the hierarchy, adding to the confusion.

Dr. Suh's Minimal Good System Axiom (Suh 1990) says that the requirements of a system must be independent of each other. This means that if one requirement is a subset of another requirement, they are not independent of each other. This causes problems when things change, as changes ripple down the hierarchy. It causes problems in stakeholders' understanding because businesspeople do not think of requirements in terms of hierarchies. It requires extensive connections and communication between teams creating requirements specifications within the hierarchy. It requires additional layers of management, as people need to be responsible for the various layers of requirements.

In reality, sometimes use cases need "groupings" in projects. There are two ways to accomplishing grouping without the ills of hierarchies.

To group use cases for *project organization reasons*, use UML packages instead of hierarchies. Here are some examples of project organization grouping:

- Use cases assigned to business analysis teams
- Use cases relating to separate product releases
- Use cases at different points in their completeness (facade, filled, focused) or maturity (demonstrable, stable)

For project organization grouping needs, use the UML *package*. The package is a dumb container of use cases (or any other UML artifact). The package never needs to be modified if the use cases within it are modified, moved, merged, or deleted. Avoid the urge to embed intelligence in the packages by making them "high level" use cases.

You may also need to group use cases to show that *multiple use cases are needed to fulfill a certain business process*. In this case, the use cases themselves should not be linked, because that would violate Suh's axiom and would also cause a lot of rework when the business process changed (which is very likely during the next downsizing, rightsizing, reorganization, or whatever). Instead, create a *scenario* (see Section 2.3.4). You may remember that a scenario is a real-life instance of a use case. In this situation, we are creating a multiuse case scenario, a scenario that links several use cases together to illustrate a full lifecycle business process (that is, the entire procurement/usage/disposal lifecycle). The scenario will be very useful to the testers, who can use it as an example for the tests they create for the business processes and computer application. Plus, it is an effective way to tell if there is a match between the system use cases and the business process definitions. The scenario is not a hierarchy of use cases. It is not a use case itself, just a temporary linkage of use cases to test assumptions.

Keep a close watch on your requirements for hierarchies. Once they appear, stamp them out. This applies to use cases, nonfunctional requirements and business rules.

NOTE: In the first edition of this book, we advocated a tool called *system context level use case*. This represented a very weak version of use case hierarchy, but a hierarchy nevertheless. Since we've seen the system context level use case cause so many problems in so many projects, we formally disavow this technique in this new edition.

NOTE: One hierarchy you will notice us using is the actor hierarchy. Actors themselves are not requirements, so putting them into a hierarchy is useful and doesn't have dire consequences.

4.3.3 Use Case Name Filters

When you're considering use case names, it's a good idea to run them through the following filters. Use case names

- Should conform to verb-noun construction: mail checks, determine eligibility, trace shipment, print letter
- Can contain adjectives or adverbs
- Should not contain any situation-specific data
- Should not be tied to an organization structure, paper forms, computer implementation, or manual process: enter form 104-B, complete approval window, get approval from immediate supervisor in Accounting Department
- Should not use "weak verbs" (discussed later) that do not describe the action: process, complete, do, track

4.3.4 Actor Filter

A single person can play multiple roles, and actors can include external systems or devices. Therefore, the names of actors that involve human actions should reflect the roles that people play and not the names of actual people. Actors get value, provide value to the system, or both. Generalizing several layers of actors is best left until the Filled iteration (discussed in Chapter 5).

Be careful not to link a use case actor to your current organization chart. Although the actor's name must be recognizable to the users, there may be a more generic or abstract name that would still make sense to the users and would not tie your use cases into the current organizational chart (see Table 4.5).

Table 4.5   Evaluating Actor Names

Good Actor Names	Poor Actor Names
Pension clerk	Clerk
Sales supervisor	Third-Level Supervisor
Production accountant	Data Entry Clerk #165
Customer service representative	Eddie "The Dawg" Taylor

4.3.5 Verb Filter

Concrete ("strong") verbs are more meaningful in use case names than are general ("weak") verbs (see Table 4.6 for examples). If you find yourself using weak verbs in use case names, it may be that you are unsure of exactly what this use case is accomplishing. You may be recording a use case that provides no value to the actor, or you may be bowing to time pressure, reducing the quality of your work.

Table 4.6   Strong and Weak Use Case Verbs

Concrete (Strong) Verbs in Use Case Names	General (Weak) Verbs in Use Case Names
Create	Make
Remove	Report
Merge	Use
Defer	Copy
Switch	Organize
Calculate	Record
Pay	Repeat
Credit	Find
Register	Process
Deactivate	Maintain
Review	Display
View	List
Enter	Retrieve
Change	Integrate
Combine	Input
Release	
Search	
Migrate	
Receive	

continues

Table 4.6   continued

Concrete (Strong) Verbs in Use Case Names	General (Weak) Verbs in Use Case Names
Debit	
Activate	
Archive	
Browse	

NOTE: In some situations, verbs we've designated as "weak" are quite acceptable, such as an industry-specific verb. For example, when a banker talks about "processing a loan," the word *process* is quite specific and therefore a good use case verb. There are always exceptions to the rules.

4.3.6 Noun Filters

Strong (concrete) nouns, like strong verbs, show that use case authors know what they are talking about and aren't hedging. Table 4.7 shows examples.

Table 4.7   Strong and Weak Use Case Nouns

Strong	Weak
Property	Data
Loan	Paper
Agent	Report
Supplies	System
Price	Form
Costs	Template
Offer	
Account	
Trend	
Date	
Sales	

4.3.7 Packages as Placeholders for Functionality

Packages can be a convenient tool for creating placeholders for large areas of functionality that are not addressed during the Facade iteration. Interactions between the unknown functional area (indicated by the package) and the rest of the system (defined in the Facade use cases) can ensure that the only thing that remains undocumented is the functionality inside the package itself.

NOTE: The principle of the Facade iteration is to write use cases to create placeholders for each functional area. Your focus must be on the functionality that is the hardest to define or the most nebulous. Therefore, it's a good idea to take a close look at those functional areas that you wish to put inside packages during this iteration. It may be important to break those packages down into Facade use cases instead of leaving them as amorphous packages. Packages are more useful when they hold a place for functionality that cannot be defined at this time or that is known to be simple and is not worth documenting now.

4.3.8 Facade Filter

At what level should Facade use cases exist? Your definition of Facade use cases must start with the major transactions of the system. Activities such as security, audit, backup, and recovery merely support the major business interactions. Leave them until late in the iteration. But there must be at least one Facade use case representing every interaction between an initiating actor (human or computer) and the application in scope.

Facade use cases should be relatively abstract. Abstract use cases can cover a variety of actual proposed interactions with just one abstract interaction. Constantine and Lockwood (1999) talk about "essential use cases," which are abstract enough to define truly how the system interacts with the user without any regard for implementation details.

Omit from this iteration all use case diagram adornments, such as *extend* or *include*. Also, there is no need to spend time on the Basic Course of Events section in the use case template. Just fill in a brief summary for each use case as a placeholder.

4.3.9 Peer Review

Think of use case *peer reviews* as code walk-throughs for use cases, except that peer reviews are much more brief. It is easy to review five use cases in one sitting. Have a technical architect present who can begin to estimate how much architecture is required by these interactions. Also, include an SME who understands the business domain. That person watches for major "gotchas" that you want to catch before you make a fool of yourself in front of the user.

Have peer reviews often and informally. Don't hesitate to pass your Facade use cases by your coworkers during this phase, or perhaps use an outside quality assurance authority. The more involvement there is by these various parties at this time, the easier the later iterations will be, and certainly the easier design and development will become.

The input is the Facade use cases, perhaps partially completed. The process is a review of the use cases for problems in nomenclature, standards, and so on. The output is improved use cases and a list of changes for the author to make. If this is the final review before user review, the output includes a deadline for making the changes.

4.3.10 User Review

User review of your Facade use cases is critical. Plan one or several face-to-face meetings (if possible) with your users to walk through the use cases. You are already iterating through your use case development (Facade, Filled, Focused), so you do not need to have multiple sessions with the same users, but you may need to schedule multiple sessions to include each user who requires involvement. Every hour you spend in user review is an investment in problem avoidance that repays you tenfold later.

4.4 Deliverables

The Facade iteration is complete when

- A system context use case is documented.
- The project manager has an 80% confidence that all Facade-level use cases have been identified.
- Every use case identified has been documented.

Some planning is required before you move on to your next use case iteration. It is during the Filled iteration that you widen your scope, deepen your analyses, and broaden your context. You will take many of the ideas that surfaced in Facade and bring them to life.

The outputs from the Facade iteration are as follows:

Problem statement	Complete
Statement of work	Complete
Risk analysis	Iterating
Use case diagrams	Iterating
Use cases	Iterating
Business rules	Iterating

4.5 Roles

Table 4.8 shows the roles that are involved in this iteration.

Table 4.8 Roles in the Facade Iteration

Role	Duties
Requirements analyst	Create Facade use cases, use case diagrams, and business rules.
Stakeholder	Participate in interviews.
Executive sponsor	Review problem statement, informal review, occasional status.
Technical architect	Attend peer reviews.
Project manager	Assist in developing the statement of work, provide updates to problem statement.

4.6 Context

The Facade iteration creates placeholders for each use case. This iteration provides a structure for the use cases to come.

4.7 Summary

Start your requirements effort with the Facade iteration. This process gives you a high-level view of the system that you are going to build, and it organizes your efforts by giving you placeholders for the tasks that remain.

To create the Facade iteration, dig into the system and talk to the stakeholders. As you build a mental image of the system, describe its components in simple use cases. When you have Facade use cases written for the major parts of the system, the work remaining for other iterations is to increase the value of each one until you have documented sufficient detail to build the system.

Several tools are at your disposal to help keep this iteration on track. The verb, use case name, and actor filters will help you avoid classic use case traps. The supporting requirements documentation (see Chapter 3), together with the Facade use cases, immediately reduces the ambiguity of what the system must do for its users, and this is the central point of requirements gathering.

5

For every problem, there is one solution which is simple, neat, and wrong.

—H. L. MENCKEN

The Filled Iteration

The Filled Iteration

5.1 Objectives

Putting together comprehensive requirements for a nontrivial application is a complex task. During the Filled iteration, you face the magnitude of this task.

5.2 Steps

To create the Filled iteration artifacts, follow these steps:

1. Break out detailed use cases.
2. Create Filled use cases.
3. Add business rules.
4. Test the Filled use cases.
5. Put some things off.

5.2.1 Break Out Detailed Use Cases

During the Facade iteration, you created use cases for each major interaction. As you delve into more detail during the Filled iteration, you will find that some of these Facade use cases are too general and need to be broken down into several Filled use cases. This challenging task poses questions such as, What size should a use case be? Where is the natural breakdown between functionality?

Before we answer these questions, let's expand step 1, breaking out detailed use cases, into more detailed steps.

1. Add detail to the use case diagrams.
2. Review use case granularity.

5.2.1.1 Add Detail to the Use Case Diagrams

You created an initial set of use case diagrams for the Facade iteration. During the Filled iteration, you take the vaguely described Facade use cases and create Filled use cases, adding any other details that are uncovered as you get into greater detail in the text use cases. There is generally a one-to-one ratio of Facade use case to Filled use case, but not always. There are often new use cases uncovered once the details come up, resulting in Filled use cases that never existed in the Facade iteration. Also, some Facade use cases may break into two or more Filled use cases (see Section 5.2.1.2).

5.2.1.2 Review Use Case Granularity

Earlier we posed the question, What size should a use case be? "Size" does not refer to the amount of documentation that supports a use case, nor does it indicate how detailed a use case should be. Rather, it refers to how you define the boundaries between system functionality. Another way to look at the issue is to ask, How do we split system functionality into use cases? How many use cases should we employ to describe the system? These are questions of *use case granularity*.

DEFINITION: Use case granularity is the relative scope of individual use cases compared to the application's scope.

You can describe a system in a few or a great many use cases. The fewer the use cases, the coarser the granularity of each use case.

Granularity is a relative measure, and there are no metrics established to determine correct granularity for all projects. Instead, you choose granularity that is appropriate for a specific development effort. Your goal in gathering requirements is to understand and communicate scope, complexity, and detail. The granularity you choose for documenting requirements must facilitate division of work among analysts and must allow ease of change. In addition, the granularity must be acceptable to your stakeholders.

The best way to finalize the granularity decision is to provide the team with guidelines and discuss the factors that guided the choices. Consistency and consensus are important criteria for successful granularity across use cases. One guideline that we've used successfully is to think of the iterations of design and development. Iterations are often set as one to three weeks. Making this assumption, think about what can be accomplished in one week (or two or three). Choose a single example of functionality and revalidate the requirements, doing analysis, design, construction, testing, and deployment. Given one of the paths (scenarios) of the use cases you've created, could your team implement it in a week? Two? Three? The answer to that question becomes a good acid test for use case granularity.

What differences will granularity make to the use cases? A too-fine granularity may not be able to provide true business value in a single use case, and that may make it difficult to grasp a business concept. A too-coarse granularity increases complexity and decreases readability.

After you have completed the initial identification of the detailed use cases, it is time to review their granularity and change it if necessary. Ask the following questions of the detailed use cases:

- Does each use case provide a sufficient "big picture" view of its functionality?
- If you broke down the use cases, would they be easier to understand?
- Can you make them easier to work on?
- If you needed to change some details in a use case, would it be difficult?
- Can one analyst work on one use case, or is it so big that two or more analysts would have to work on it?
- Could a reasonably sized team take one path (scenario) from the use case from requirements to deployment in one, two, or three weeks?

When you have found a granularity that works well, apply it also to the use case diagram. Group related use cases into packages, and draw a use case diagram for each package. The system context use case diagram shows the big picture, and each package's diagram will contain the detail for each set of use cases.

After you implement any changes due to granularity, review the use cases and their summaries to ensure that you have not omitted considerations of scope. Name and summarize any additional use cases, and then update the use case diagram. You will complete these use cases, so it is important to identify all the necessary use cases as placeholders at this time.

5.2.2 Create Filled Use Cases

Now that you have summarized all the use cases in the application (we hope!), you are ready to build each one. Because you have chosen an appropriate granularity, you can safely take the time to build the detailed use cases.

Stakeholder meetings have formed the input into most of these steps. If more information is needed, head back to the stakeholders to confirm, probe, and query.

The following sections show the steps for completing the Filled use cases.

5.2.2.1 Identify Triggers

A use case *trigger* is the impulse or event that initiates the use case.

Triggers answer the questions, When does this use case start? What impulse or event signaled the start of this use case? A use case may have more than one trigger. To help discover all the triggers, ask the stakeholder to describe the process flow.

Describe the trigger in the active voice ("The build manager asks the developer to build a product release") rather than the passive voice ("The developer is asked to build a product release"), and state the condition simply. Do not describe the trigger in terms of the software system; instead, relate it to the business being modeled. For example, a use case should not start when a user opens a window; instead, it should start when a sales agent receives a telephone order.

Clarify whether a trigger is also an automation requirement. For example, suppose that a trigger for a use case that captures a telephone purchase order is "Sales agent receives a telephone call." The problem with this description is that it does not specify whether the telephone or the sales agent triggered the use case. Talk to the stakeholders about the level of automation they require, and document it clearly to avoid this kind of ambiguous requirement. In such a discussion, it is useful to distinguish between "possible but expensive" versus "realistic" requirements.

Here are examples of triggers:

- The build manager asks the developer to build a product release.
- The system detects a work file in the inbound processing queue.

5.2.2.2 Identify Preconditions

Preconditions describe a mandatory state of the system at the inception of the use case.

A precondition is anything that the use case assumes has occurred before its starting point that is relevant to the use case. Describe the business conditions that must precede use case initiation. Ask the stakeholder questions such as, What must happen before we can do this? What do you need to have before you can perform this functionality?

Examine the inputs to the use case—whether the input is a piece of information (such as a form) or an event (such as someone retiring)—and ask how this use case will be aware of it. For example, suppose that in your use case, the actor keys data. Ask where the data came from. If it is mailed and if this is the first time the system comes into contact with it, then a precondition is that the data entry sheets are available. A related trigger could be that at least ten data entry forms have accumulated.

Preconditions and use case triggers are related. Together, they describe the state of the system when the use case starts. The difference between a precondition and a trigger is that satisfying the preconditions is not, by itself, a sufficient condition to initiate the use case, the trigger will provide the impetus to start the use case, and that initialization will be successful only if the preconditions have also been satisfied. All preconditions must be satisfied for the trigger to be able to initiate the use case.

Also note that a condition should not be included in both the precondition and the exception area of a use case. If the condition is included in both, you have introduced redundancy. The exception cannot occur because the use case would not begin until the condition was satisfied.

Another use case, an actor, or a system actor must be capable of satisfying all preconditions of any use case.

5.2.2.3 Refine the Use Case Name

The *name* of a use case describes the primary actor's objective. This is a noun-verb combination.

Ask the stakeholder to define the most important objective of the use case. Answering this question is difficult, so encourage the user to explore the possibilities and to examine the use case's completion criteria. One area that confuses users when discussing objectives is this: From whose perspective should the objective be considered?

For example, in a book-ordering system, the customer's criterion for use case completion is that she receive the book that she ordered. From the perspective of the sales clerk, the objective is to collect the order, address, and payment information and to send the order to the dispatching warehouse.

The use case name should reflect the objective of the primary actor. In our example, the sales clerk is the primary actor, and the customer is a secondary actor, so the use case name should be *Create Sales Order*. To avoid confusion when you name use cases, discuss with the stakeholder which of the actors is the primary one. In addition to helping you identify a good use case name, gaining a clear understanding of the objectives will improve all areas of the use case.

Section 4.3 describes several tools that help in this process, including a use case name filter that helps you avoid using weak use case names.

5.2.2.4 Refine the Actors

The use case *actor* is an abstraction of any role that interacts with the use case.

The use case diagram indicates the roles that interact with a use case as actors. These are the stick-figure people attached to the use cases. Each actor is a role and can represent a person or a system.

It is important that you understand "who does what" in each use case. Ask the stakeholder questions such as What roles are involved in this task? How do they interact? To prevent confusion regarding similar roles, collect any relevant information about each actor in an actor profile. For example, if an actor is someone who sometimes works remotely, record this in the profile.

5.2.2.5 Specify the Basic Course of Events

The Basic Course of Events section of a use case specifies the actor's interactions with the system and with other actors to achieve the actor's goals. The events tell a story that describes how a triggered use case progresses toward its objective and the steps in between.

Write the basic course of events as numbered instructions that tell the actor what to do and that show how the system responds.

For example, let's say that during the Facade iteration, a use case called *Enter Tenant Details* (see Appendix A) has the following summary and little other information:

The system stores a set of details about each tenant (lease holder).

In Use Case 5.1, we add the Basic Course of Events. Each statement in the Basic Course of Events section is part of the dialog between the actor and the system. This section describes the straight line through the process; variations and exceptions have their own section. The information in the basic course of events comes from your interview with the stakeholders. Have the stakeholders describe how they envision the actor achieving the objectives of the use case. Ask them to list all the steps that they can think of. This information will give you the first cut at the course of events. Go into detail for these steps. If they say, "We enter the customer's demographics," ask them to elaborate on these details. Ask, What happens if . . . ? If there are multiple actors in a use case, ask, Who does what? Don't be afraid to ask persistent questions. Repeat the interviews to clarify any details that remain obscure.

If there is an existing system or manual process, it makes it easier for the stakeholders to give you the detail needed for these steps. If there is no existing system, encourage them to imagine it and to think of all the detail they need for the process. Walk the stakeholders through the steps to encourage them to remember additional details.

The Basic Course of Events section must expose complex processes and reveal simple, easily read steps. To "open the black box" and make the process clear is your goal for writing this section. Aim to elaborate a process sufficiently to reveal all its intricacies.

Avoid naming user interface controls in the steps. Always translate the requirement into a format that excludes GUI specifics, and ask the stakeholder for the underlying requirement. For example, don't write, "Click the OK button." Instead, write, "Save the demographic details."

TIP: Maintain a glossary of all the business terms included in the use cases. The glossary should explain the terms used and has the dual function of clarifying and confirming your use of the specific terms. This action reduces jargon confusion between stakeholders and analysts during the requirements-gathering activity, and it clarifies your use cases to the designers.

Use Case:	**Enter Tenant Details**
Description:	The real estate system tracks who is leasing a property; the system stores a set of details of each tenant (lease holder) for billing, tracking, and exposure reasons.
Triggers:	A new tenant or potential tenant has been found for a property lease—this could be initiated from the lease property use case.
	Additional or changed information has been found for an existing tenant.
Basic Course of Events:	1. The actor navigates to the tenant area. 2. The actor enters the identification information for a tenant. 3. First name, last name, and SSN are entered for an individual; or 4. Company name and federal tax ID for an institution or organization. 5. The system checks for existing matching entries. 6. The system displays a data entry template that is populated with any existing information. The template differs for individuals and organizations. 7. \<list of data items\>. 8. The actor enters each data item. 9. The system validates data according to the data entry rules (dates, etc.). 10. When satisfied with the data entry the actor commits the changes. 11. The system validates that the data set is complete. 12. The system stores the changes, and if validation passed the tenant is marked as validated.

Use Case 5.1   *Enter Tenant Details*

5.2.2.6 Indicate Repetition

Repetition is the reiteration of a process by an actor until a condition changes.

The basic course of events must often show repeating steps as well as alternative paths and exception paths. Use a tiered numbering scheme to indicate repetition. For example:

1. Indicate customer's color choice from the set displayed.
2. (Optional) Indicate as many as five alternative choices.
3. Go on to the next step.

Ask, What is the condition for ending the repetition? Will there be the same number of repetitions each time? Then translate the answers into the requirements that the user interface designers and data designers must know. Additionally, this information is valuable for defining scope.

5.2.2.7 Document Exceptions

Exceptions specify the actor's interactions with the system, and with other actors, when the basic course of events is not followed.

The exceptions and alternatives listed in Use Case 5.2 apply to the Basic Course of Events section of Use Case 5.1.

The exceptions have their own section in the use case template, immediately below the Basic Course of Events section. If there is ambiguity regarding which step the exception relates to, clarify by referring to the step's number. If the description of the exception requires multiple statements, use tiered numbering like that used in the Basic Course of Events section. The default is to return to the next event statement; if that is not the default, show the event number to return to. If an exception ends a use case, state it.

Write your use cases so that all levels of users are comfortable reading them. When you are writing exceptions, avoid the use of IF-THEN-ELSE construction. Such pseudocode breaks the flow of the use case story, and executive-level users may not be comfortable with it. Write exceptions so that they can be read naturally, and do not capitalize words such as *otherwise*.

The Basic Course of Events section specifies the straight line through from trigger to use case completion. This is the basic process. Most use cases have exceptions in response to specific circumstances. We document these because the system must be able to handle them. Exceptions document the answers to the range of questions that begin with, What will the actor do if . . . ?

Exceptions:	3. If the system finds a duplicate, alter the actor and display the existing tenant record.
	8. If mandatory data is missing, the system alerts the actor and explains the omission. If the tenant refers to a current lessee (that is, a tenant with an active lease), and the system will not accept changes, that will cause the tenant to lose validation status.
	7. If the actor is not satisfied with the changes, the actor optionally may abandon the changes. The system reverts to the previously stored record if one existed.

Use Case 5.2   *Exceptions and Alternatives Sections of Use Case 5.1*

Identify the business process exceptions to respond to real-world inputs; do not document possible software exceptions. To identify the relevant exception, discover how the actor should interact with the system when the process deviates from typical processing. In this way, the use case can describe the interaction between actors and the system that accomplishes real business. Ask the stakeholder what-happens-if questions to discover the exceptions. But be sure to distinguish between exceptions and improbable occurrences. The focus of most business development is to create a system that functions correctly for the majority of the business cases that it handles. Typically, the system designers decide not to explicitly handle every possible business exception. Embedded systems and mission-critical systems may need to handle a larger set of improbable conditions. As with the majority of the rules surrounding use cases, you are free to make and break them as you choose.

When Should You Make an Exception into a New Use Case?

While writing use cases, guard against creating a use case that is too large to be managed. When the size of an exception is comparable to that of the use case, it can be a warning signal that the exception, even if it appears to be related to the use case, should be a separate use case.

If your exception is too large or if it has exceptions of its own, create a separate use case for it. At this point do not relate it to other use cases with *include* and *extend* relationships. Do this in the next iteration.

5.2.2.8 Refine the Use of Language

It sounds basic, but grammar and spelling in your use cases are important. Use cases are written in natural language, so the only syntax that guides you when writing them is the use of language. You can be sure that your work will be judged on the quality of the writing in the use cases as much as anything else.

In general, use the active voice ("The actor did it") rather than the passive voice ("It was done by the actor"). Writing in the passive voice may be a clue that information is missing. If you're saying, "It was done," without specifying who did it, perhaps it is time to find out who did it.

Also, try to keep technical jargon out of your use cases.

5.2.3 Add Business Rules

Collect the business rules in parallel with developing the use cases and identifying the non-functional requirements. During the Filled iteration, you are simply adding business rules as they appear during use case creation. At this point there is no need to comply with strict formats or categorizations for business rules. You can apply these in later iterations.

5.2.4 Test the Filled Use Cases

After you have built the use cases, check their completeness and quality. Because the use cases are not ready to be examined by the stakeholders, this should be an internal review. It is for your benefit only. It allows you to identify vague points in your use cases and to return to the stakeholders for clarification.

Employ scenarios for testing use cases. Chapter 2 defines a scenario as a possible path through a use case. Create a scenario by choosing data that will drive a use case through a specific set of main flow and exception statements.

Apply a scenario by reading each step, supplying data to it, and obeying the use case's rules. Applying a scenario allows you to walk through a use case by following the flow and exceptions dictated by the data. This process helps you identify missing steps and discover additional exceptions, and that makes it a useful tool for quality-checking your work.

Each use case may have many possible scenarios. You may want to create scenario data for the normal processing scenario and for the more important exceptions. Scenarios do not have to be formalized or recorded to be an effective testing tool.

While you walk through a scenario, ask whether the use case documents the modeled system sufficiently. Test a use case comprehensively by executing a scenario for each path in the use case. Check that the exceptions are called and that the use case handles each exception.

Scenarios can be used to test both system requirements and the finished product. If you do formalize a scenario, it will be useful to the testing team. See Appendix A for additional detail on how to leverage your use case efforts throughout the software development lifecycle.

> **Helping Users Help You Test a Use Case**
>
> How do you guide users through testing a use case, given the differences between use cases and scenarios?
>
> When a user is explaining to you the rules from which a business process executes, both of you can experience a great deal of ambiguity because of the differences in how each of you views the events. The interviewer tends to ask the questions in use case language, and the interviewee tends to provide answers in "scenario land." Business users typically describe the set of circumstances in which they find themselves. If they have a specialty within the business process being described, their descriptions of the straight line path and the exceptions will reflect it. Under these circumstances, the dialog is likely to be misleading.
>
> Be especially aware of the potential for this problem when the user is describing scenarios without first describing the main path and listing the exceptions. For example, if the business user says, "The customer calls to verify the order that was received via the Web," this is a danger sign. It is possible that the conditions described actually reflect an exception and not the main flow. Ask questions to determine whether this is so and to determine the additional paths that the business process could follow.

5.2.5 Put Some Things Off

Certain tasks should be put off until later iterations. The Filled iteration is the time to expand the detail of the documented requirements but not to increase or decrease the scope dramatically. It is good to wait on the following tasks:

- Identifying common behavior and merging use cases
- Handling software exceptions

Above all, keep working on gathering *what* and not *how*. Keeping this focus can be difficult because describing the *how* alleviates people's fear that they are being misunderstood or the fear that the system will not match their expectations. When you are given a description that includes a *how* component, look for the reason it was expressed during requirements gathering. Perhaps an additional nonfunctional requirement lurks behind the veil of design assumptions. For example, suppose that a requirement is expressed as follows:

When the user has entered the salary, interest rate, and credit rating, the system stores the profile and calculates a band of possible loan amounts. The calculation must be performed on the server and never on the client.

Note that the last line of this requirement contains *how* information. A design decision has been expressed. If you inquire further into this statement, you may discover that the user community is worried that the calculation will not be made quickly because a previous legacy system performed the calculation on a client machine, which took several minutes. The unstated nonfunctional requirement is actually that the calculation result be returned to the user within, say, three seconds.

Here's another example:

The data system passes the Social Security number to the imaging system via API calls that will bring up the folder of personal information about the account holder through which the user can browse.

The specific *how* elements in this requirement are the mention of API calls and the use of Social Security numbers as a unique identity in an imaging system. Further conversation with this user may indicate that he wants it documented that the imaging system is integrated with his business system and that he will not have to invoke the imaging system manually to search for an account. It is a simple step to remove the unique key and API references from this requirement and still describe the interaction successfully.

Also, do not worry about the user interface requirements at this point. The way the application presents or accepts information to and from the users (the *how*) is a detail that should wait until a later iteration.

5.3 Tools

There are a number of tools (techniques and approaches) that you can employ to ease the tasks involved in the Filled iteration. Let's look at each of them in turn.

5.3.1 The Stakeholder Interview

The stakeholder interview is your primary tool for gathering requirements and for getting additional information about confusing requirements. Refer to Chapter 4 for details on interviewing stakeholders and holding joint requirements planning sessions.

5.3.2 IPA Filter

IPA stands for includes, preconditions, and assumptions (and not India Pale Ale).
    There are three parts of a use case that can be easily confused:

- An *include* association between use cases
- A *precondition* on a given use case
- An *assumption* for a use case

When should you use each of these elements? Table 5.1 lists our rules of thumb for the types of information that should populate each of these fields.

Table 5.1   Includes, Preconditions, and Assumptions Compared

Use This	Under These Conditions
Include association	When the reused use case does not provide value to an actor and it is only an intermediate step that is used by use cases within this development effort that really provide the value, it signifies an include relationship.
Precondition	When something inside the system being built, but outside this use case, must be in place before this use case can run, it is an example of a precondition.
Assumption	When something outside the control of this development effort (especially things that have been ruled beyond the scope of this project) must be in place before this use case can run, you've found an assumption.

5.3.3 White Space Analysis Filter

Think of *white space analysis filter* as a way to examine a "day in the life" (although it may refer to any period—say, a month or a year—in the life). When you walk through the existing or newly modeled business processes, you can discover that there are missing interactions, perhaps significant areas that have not been addressed in the use cases so far. We call these unaddressed areas the *white space* in your requirements picture. If this system is part of a business process engineering effort, the business process definitions can help structure the discussions. Or, if this system is automating existing procedures, those process definitions can be used. Or, more likely, the information stored in people's heads can guide the process.

Go through a day in the life of each actor, and then move on to end-of-week, end-of-month, end-of-quarter, and end-of-year processes. These walk-throughs should help you identify interactions that may not have been obvious earlier.

5.3.4 Abstraction Filter

When you're gathering requirements and making them understandable to all the stakeholders, an important function is *abstraction*. Abstraction is a process of generalization that allows you to consider the similarity between requirements and to make decisions consistently across the business domain. Take a reality check on how abstract the use cases are. The primary reason for modeling requirements with use cases is to communicate the requirements to the users, application designers, and testers. If the use cases are too abstract, they will not provide sufficient, meaningful detail. If they are not abstract enough, you will repeat similar information in many different places, resulting in problems with consistency and documentation volume.

Read your use cases and think about the various people who must rely on them. Have you provided sufficient detail, or are the use cases too abstract? Have a sample use case reviewed by a user and by an application designer. Then discuss the use case with them to ensure that they are comfortable with the level of abstraction.

5.3.5 Testing Use Cases with Scenarios

The way to attack use case testing is to use scenarios. Scenarios, discussed earlier in Section 5.2.4, are effective testing tools for use cases because they help users and IT staff walk through what would happen in an everyday interaction with the application.

5.3.6 Review

Peer reviews and user reviews should conclude this iteration to identify existing issues with the documentation.

5.3.7 Additional Use Cases

There are peripheral use cases that are often forgotten in requirements gathering.

- *Security*—authentication and authorization of users
- *Audit*—logs of online or batch activity
- *Backup and Recovery*—creating and maintaining copies of the system data
- *Remote users*—interactions of customers or supply chain partners
- *Reporting requirements*—queries and reports

The Filled iteration is the time to create these use cases.

5.4 Deliverables

The deliverables from the Filled iteration are as follows:

Candidate use case list	Partially complete
Use cases	Filled level
Use case diagrams	Filled level
Business rules catalog	Partially complete
Scenarios	Several for each use case tested

5.5 Roles

Table 5.2 shows the roles that participate in the Filled iteration.

Table 5.2   Roles in the Filled Iteration

Role	Duties
Requirements analyst	Adds detail to use cases and business rules, reinterviews stakeholders to validate earlier assumptions, documents Filled use cases
Stakeholder	Participates in interviews
Executive sponsor	Reviews occasional status update
Technical architect	Helps determine nonfunctional requirements
Project manager	Provides statement of work updates and problem statement updates

5.6 Context

During the Filled iteration, you emphasize broadening and deepening the requirements specification. During the next iteration, which we call Focused, you will concentrate on narrowing the scope and level of detail that will be most helpful to the designers and developers.

5.7 Summary

In the Filled iteration you deal with the meat of requirements gathering, when you ask questions, write use cases, and have the majority of your contact with the system stakeholders. When this iteration is complete, you will have collected sufficient information to describe the system. For many projects, design can start from use cases like the ones you create in this iteration.

6

A man is rich in proportion to the things he can afford to let alone.

—Henry David Thoreau

Focused Iteration

The Focused Iteration

6.1 Objectives

Arranged in your computer is a collection of use case documents, and each one describes a possible system component. This set of requirements may be discouragingly large. You must now select the best options identified during the Filled iteration and include only these in the project scope.

The Focused iteration clears a path through the paperwork and leaves you with clear project requirements. At the end of this iteration, you will have defined the system and will have gathered sufficient information to build a successful application.

The Focused iteration separates the *essential* from the *nice-to-have*. It is now that you decide what is important, what will be built, and why. You examine the business problem from the context of your proposed solution, and you make sure that the solution doesn't solve unnecessary problems. For this reason, the Focused iteration is a difficult one.

109

When this iteration is complete, the use case model will describe the users' interactions with the system. These interactions allow the users to solve the business problems that initiated this development effort. The deliverables you create during the Focused iteration give you a detailed understanding of the scope of the system as well as its complexity and the risks involved.

To build systems that fulfill users' needs, you must understand the essential core functionality and help them understand which functionality is necessary. You can eliminate waste by carefully examining the scope and thus reduce the system to its essentials. Removing functionality at this stage is a real money saver. You avoid the effort of prototyping, designing, reviewing, building, and testing the additional functionality.

The following sections describe the steps in the Focused iteration.

6.2 What Are Focused Use Cases?

Focused use cases build on the work you have performed thus far. You make difficult choices about the current project, decide on the feature set, determine the scope, and eliminate duplication.

Focused use cases describe the users' interaction with a system. You hone each interaction to provide a solution to a limited set of business problems. At this point, you have analyzed the business sufficiently to remove contradictory requirements and to describe from a business perspective how the use cases share functionality and assist one another in reaching an understood goal. This varies considerably from the output of the Filled iteration. Focused use cases are clear and crisp. There is no additional detail, and the focus of the system is apparent.

6.3 Steps

To create the Focused iteration artifacts, follow these steps:

1. Merge duplicate processes.
2. Bring focus to each use case.
3. Manage scope changes during this iteration.
4. Manage risks and assumptions.
5. Review.

6.3.1 Merge Duplicate Processes

Examine the contents of each use case in relation to the remaining use cases. If you can share a process with other use cases, you reduce the scope of the project. To reduce the number of use cases, you merge duplicates, generalizing similar use cases. To reduce the size of individual use cases, you merge duplicate processes and generalize processes.

The Payback of Merging Duplicate Processes

The detection and merger of duplicate processes enhances your ability to perform a number of tasks, including the following:

- Choosing better candidate use cases.
- Simplifying the application documentation.
- Prioritizing use cases.
- Creating accurate estimates. If a use case can be used elsewhere, you can estimate the work effort more accurately.
- Improving your development process. For example, if a core set of use cases is employed diversely throughout the system, it might be economical to develop an automated system to test and regression-test these use cases.
- Planning project iterations.

Many processes in a business are essentially the same. Early discovery of these similar processes in the development lifecycle will prevent you from designing, building, and testing duplicate code.

To find and remove duplicates, follow these steps:

1. Identify duplicates.
2. Split the duplicated piece into its own use case.
3. Update the use case diagram.

Merger of duplicates is crucial in this iteration. Duplicate functionality in use cases is a serious problem when you begin to implement the requirements in code. It also complicates maintenance because a single change means that you may have to update several processes.

6.3.2 Bring Focus to Each Use Case

Analysts, designers, architects, project managers, testers, technical writers, and programmers rely on use cases. In addition to extracting scope information from them, these individuals need sufficient data to be able to build and test the system. Each use case must be complete, accurate, and concise. In the Focused iteration, you edit each use case to make sure that your descriptions are complete and provide sufficient information without being wasteful or vague. You must ensure that you define the terms used for the business domain and that you have accurately defined the actors.

For this task, look into the following:

- *Interfaces to other systems (ports, APIs, telephony, Internet, and so on)*—Have you neglected any of these?
- *The relationships between the interfaces and the use cases*—For example, can the telephony interface provide the necessary services to each of the use cases that depend on it?

- *Improving the processes*—Walk through each of the processes from the point of view of the user. What does this tell you about the process? Have you inadvertently retained the manual process? If you have, is it efficient enough for the future system?
- *Prioritizing the use cases*—Have you numbered them in order of importance and urgency to the users? This helps you to identify which use cases should be in the early design and development increments and stages of delivery.
- *Defining the inputs and outputs*—Examine these with the processes to ensure that you have not missed something.

6.3.3 Manage Scope Changes During This Iteration

Requirements change. This moving target, often called *scope creep*, is invariably viewed as negative. Change renders your carefully crafted requirements obsolete, and that is frustrating. But businesses and government agencies are judged on their ability to adapt to their chaotic marketplaces, so their software must be able to change with them, even while it is being created. Given that you have no totalitarian solution to abolish changes, you must accept change during requirements analysis as well as during the rest of application development. You can develop strategies that allow you to cope with such changes.

When change occurs, you must evaluate its consequences objectively and implement them sensibly. Change may increase or decrease scope. Dealing with a scope decrease—a change that reduces the level of automation in a system—might seem easier. However, it is important that you apply the same mechanisms to analyze both types of changes. Your goal is to identify how a change may alter the system. Dependencies between use cases are relevant to the task of understanding change.

Strategies for Change

Your objective is to handle scope and requirement changes flexibly and accurately. The key is to understand how the overall system must adapt to accommodate the change.

Introducing a new use case typically causes less change than does altering existing use cases. Discovering how the change influences existing functionality accounts for the majority of the effort.

The user community must be involved in defining the additional functionality. We have found it beneficial to walk through the full requirements lifecycle with the additional functionality. Start by defining the Facade iteration of the additional use case. If you are in the position of suggesting change control, you should use the Facade version of the additional use case as the vehicle with which to propose the change. The format is suitable because all the stakeholders are familiar with it. It is also quick to put together, and it is reasonable for inclusion into the matrix. During this process, you should be receptive to the possibility that a new use case may not be required. If possible, it's best to generalize existing functionality to meet the additional requirements.

6.3.4 Manage Risks and Assumptions

While working on this iteration, you'll discover facets of the system that may not be appropriate content for a use case. Even though these observations are irrelevant to requirements gathering, it is important to record and communicate them to team members and users.

Carefully document the assumptions that underlie your requirements. The system and its scope may change significantly if these assumptions fail. For this reason, you should present the assumptions to the users with your use cases.

The following are some of the risks of the Focused iteration:

- Neglect of a major requirement
- Overengineering of use cases
- A user group that is not comfortable with the use cases

You can control these risks by being aware of them during this iteration. Make sure that your reviewers are aware of the risks so that they can screen the requirements for these problems. If the users are not comfortable with their understanding of use cases, it is worth the effort to educate a representative user and involve him or her actively in the requirements-gathering process.

We recommend an active approach to risk management. For example, to mitigate and manage project risk we use the strategy proposed in *Rapid Development: Taming Wild Software Schedules* (McConnell 1996).

6.3.5 Review

It is essential that somebody review your work for this iteration. Ideal candidates for reviewers are the SMEs because they have the best understanding of the business and the emerging application.

Reviewers look at use cases individually and as a part of the completed system. Each use case must be reviewed for accuracy and completeness. The reviewer must ascertain that the collection of use cases describes an adequate system.

If you are reviewing the Focused iteration, what do you look for?

6.3.5.1 Identify Opportunities Not Taken

In reviewing the work done in the Focused iteration, you may be able to identify areas where further possibilities remain. Ask yourself the following questions:

- Is there duplicate functionality in the system?
- Do the use cases include unnecessary functionality?
- Are any of the processes overly complex?
- Can the team make improvements?
- Is the level of detail and refinement consistent across use cases developed by different teams and team members? (It is important to consider some of the challenges imposed by teamwork on this process.)

6.3.5.2 System Damage

Watch for the following types of faults. You may be reviewing your own or the team's use cases, or you may be a client reviewing the work of an outsourcer.

- Have we inadvertently removed essential parts of the system?
- Will shared functionality work correctly for both processes?
- Does the set of use cases describe a system that meets the business criteria that have prompted this project?
- Does the set of use cases describe a system that meets known technical requirements?
- Have any references to a specific technology crept in?
- Has there been any attempt to design the system at this point?

In addition to looking for mistakes and omissions in the use cases, you should examine the risk and assumptions documentation and be alert for unidentified risks. You should make detailed comments on all flaws to the requirements analyst. The analyst needs to incorporate the observations and correct any defects found.

Reacting to the Review

If you're the requirements analyst and some of your changes do not make it through the review, how will it affect you? If the review returns previously rejected functionality to the system, have the reviewer prioritize its importance. During project planning, it is helpful to know which requirements are essential to the system and which are cosmetic.

6.4 Tools

A number of tools are available for your use in the Focused iteration. Let's look at each of them in turn.

6.4.1 Surplus Functionality Filter

Reduce scope in this iteration by examining each use case in relation to the system objective. Remove use cases that are tangential to these objectives. Examine each use case in isolation and remove details or features that are not required.

6.4.2 Narrow the Focus of the System

Now it's time to examine the set of use cases for an odd one out. Look for a use case or set of use cases that does not fit well with the remainder of the system. This use case may represent a subsystem that you can identify as a separate project. Look for noncore use cases that core use cases do not use.

*The Focused iteration is about pruning requirements
detail, duplicates, conflicts, and scope.*

Until your team understands the use cases, avoid the temptation to reduce functionality. Present your findings to the users; it is essential to involve the user community in these decisions.

6.4.3 Identify Surplus Functionality Inside the Use Case

How do you identify surplus functionality? Each use case contains a short description; you should compare the body of the use case to this description to see where additional functionality is being introduced.

This technique is analogous to the comparison you performed between each use case and the system description.

When you suspect that functionality in the use case is excessive, the next step is to decide whether the users can do without it. If they can, it is safe to remove the functionality. If the users need it and if the functionality really is a bad fit for the use case, it is reasonable to move it elsewhere, either to a new use case or into an existing use case. In either case, it has an effect on the dependency relationships to the system. After altering the system, update the matrix. This update is especially important when people are working in teams. The matrix is a communication mechanism that prevents other team members from repeating your work.

6.4.4 Vocabulary Filter

Another important technique in the Focused iteration is to examine your use of proprietary names. For example, a list of requirements that we saw a few years ago stated that the application must provide a Soundex search capability. Soundex was invented in the late 1800s as a means of identifying lost characters in telegram transmissions. Since then, it has been made obsolete (as you might guess) by a number of cheaper, better technology solutions. Did the requirements analyst really want to specify such outdated technology? Perhaps the analyst meant a *sound-alike feature* or some other nonproprietary feature.

6.5 Deliverables

The deliverables of the Focused iteration include the following:

Problem statement	Complete
Statement of work	Complete
Use cases	Focused level
Use case diagrams	Focused level
Business rule catalog	Almost complete
Risk analysis	Ongoing
Prototype	Not started

6.6 Roles

Table 6.1 shows the roles involved in the Focused iteration.

6.7 Context

During the Focused iteration you reduce the volume of specifications somewhat by making the documentation more efficient. You also bring focus to the dependencies between use cases to help identify what is happening when scope changes.

Table 6.1   Roles in the Focused Iteration

Role	Duties
Requirements analyst	Consolidates use cases and business rules, reinterviewing stakeholders to validate earlier assumptions; documents Focused use cases
Stakeholder	Participates in interviews
Executive sponsor	Requires an occasional status update
Technical architect	Refines nonfunctional requirements; participates in reviews
Project manager	Refines problem statement and statement of work

During the next iteration, you will put final touches on the documentation and refine it until it is suitable for the designers and developers, who will use it in later activities.

6.8 Summary

To meet the challenges of the Focused iteration, you must carefully analyze use cases individually and as a whole. Your goal is to ensure that each of the use cases you will carry into the Finished iteration is efficiently written and describes a necessary task in solving the business problem. You also identify all the dependencies between use cases and consolidate them wherever possible.

7

What Skipper would

Incur the risk,

What Buccaneer would ride,

Without a surety from the wind

Or schedule of the tide?

—EMILY DICKINSON

Managing Requirements and People

Sea Captain Taking Note of His Charts

7.1 Introduction

The perceived importance of project management has been increasing in the years since Peter Drucker (Drucker 1993) introduced it as a topic worthy of discussion and specialization in the 1950s. Management of software development projects has also been a much discussed area. It is fair to say software development projects are among the most complex undertakings. It is also fair to say that they have consistently been poorly managed, given the rate of success of projects in our industry (http://www.standishgroup.com/) versus projects in other industries.

119

We all understand that a lack of good project managers is a problem. The Project Management Institute (PMI) (http://www.pmi.org) was founded to create a "profession" of project management, much like the professions of accounting, law, or medicine. This has been a fantastic positive step for advancing project management knowledge and prestige.

In this chapter, we will examine why software projects are managed poorly, where we believe the problems come from, and what some possible solutions are. Considering this is a book about requirements for software, this may seem to be an overreaching goal for this chapter. However, we believe the requirements activity and project management have become increasingly intertwined. In the past, project managers have held themselves away from specific scope issues and managed more with work breakdown structures, timesheets, task lists, and issue logs. As we've progressed as an industry, we have evolved into a new style of project management that recognizes the "management importance" of requirements activities.

First, we'll examine the existing ways of project management. Then we'll look at the improvements teams are making to manage more effectively, complementing the changes in the requirements process.

7.2 Waterfall Lifecycle Management

Walker Royce (Royce 1998) states that the "waterfall" lifecycle is less the twenty-first century's "conventional" software lifecycle and more the "benchmark" for newer lifecycle models. By benchmark, we mean that waterfall is something for us to compare new lifecycle models back to. You might think Walker wants to maintain the importance of the waterfall lifecycle because his father, Winston Royce, contributed significantly to it in the 1970s. This might be partially the case, but we feel Walker is right on target with his observation. But first, let's examine what the waterfall lifecycle represents.

Waterfalls—Beautiful in Nature, Lousy in Software Development

Table 7.1 Advantages of Waterfall

The detailed scope of the project is nailed down early in the project allowing the remaining tasks to be based on a stable set of requirements.
The project team can create "economies of scale" throughout the lifecycle, producing analysis models all at once, test executions all at once, etc.
Project managers can create clear deadlines for each activity; they know when each needs to be done in order to meet the end deadline.
There is no expensive rework; going back to previous phases is not allowed.
Staffing is predictable; more business analysts are required at the beginning; more programmers and testers in the middle; and more deployment specialists, technical writers, and trainers near the end.
Industry baselines can be created, which give standard breakdowns of how long each activity should take. For instance, requirements and analysis should take no longer than, say, 14% of the total lifecycle. If they take any longer, then it is unlikely the team will be able to meet the deadline at the end.

When the term *waterfall* is used in software development, it refers to a way of developing software that proceeds through one activity at a time, completes it fully, then moves on to the next. This has a strong set of advantages, which caused a mass adoption in the 1970s, 1980s, and 1990s.

After using waterfall for many years, we began to run up against a strong set of disadvantages, which tends to outweigh the positives. These disadvantages stemmed from the fact that the waterfall model did not satisfy what businesspeople expected from projects.

7.2.1 Nell and the Coffee Shop

Put yourself in the position of a businessperson for a minute. Let's say you are the owner of a small coffee shop. You are an especially sharp coffee shop owner. You know that investments in technology can pay off in increased business if you pick the right ones and use them intelligently and long enough to recover your initial investment.

One day, a young lady named Nell walks into your coffee shop and tells you she can provide a software system that will increase your business during slow times by 50%. She certainly has your attention. She explains the concept of the system to you and you realize that it could possibly work. Now the question is, how much? The price she quotes is reasonable, but you push her off. First, you need to crunch some numbers to determine if the investment in this system will pay back in a reasonable time, let's say within one year. The numbers come out looking good, full payback in nine months. Next, as a businessperson,

The Coffee Shop

you try to negotiate a lower price with Nell for the system. After all, payback in seven months is better than payback in eight, right? Surprisingly to you, Nell agrees, but does not negotiate a compensatory reduction in the system to accommodate the reduction in price. She just gets an annoyed, worried look on her face and accepts the deal. Oh well, it is always nice to get something for nothing, you think.

Nell says the system will be ready in one month. Perfect, you say, because in one month there will be a lot of tourists coming in for the annual festival. Increasing business during slow times with all those tourists around will mean a lot more money in a short time.

First, she interviews you quite extensively to understand how your business runs and how the system will need to work to give you the gains you need. You're impressed. She is skillful at getting to the core business issues that drive profitability and that cause the slow times. Then she explains that she will be gone for the rest of the month, designing, developing, and testing the software system to be ready by the deadline. So far, so good.

Nell is gone for only about three days before you realize you forgot to mention an important fact about the coffee shop that may help her. You call her and explain this fact, but you're surprised at her response. She says it is too late to introduce changes; only the information discussed in those interviews was relevant. Everything else will have to wait until "version two." You are not sure about the impact of this new fact, but in order to keep a good relationship with Nell, you back off. She talks about "*changecontrolmanagement*" or some such thing. Okay, okay.

After a week and a half, you are talking to a customer and she tells you about the coffee shop two streets away that has begun to offer ice cream as well as coffee, in anticipation of the tourists. The combination of coffee and ice cream is the newest wrinkle in coffee service; everyone's doing it. You think about it, and you realize that you could get the freezer in, set up the supplier relationships, and hire new staff in time to quickly add ice cream to your offerings. Oh, almost forgot about Nell! You give Nell a call to tell her about the changed situation, quite proud of yourself for thinking to include her. This time her response is even more severe. She says it is impossible to incorporate the ice cream part of your business into the system and still meet the one-month deadline. She gives you an estimate of two months to do the complete system for coffee and ice cream. Two months? The tourists will be long gone by then. Isn't there some other way?

Nell, ever the vigilant project manager, says that she can't wring blood from a stone, something has to give. You can't have all these features, by this deadline, for this price.

At first you're upset, but then you go over her words one more time. All these features, by this deadline, for this price. What a relief! You realize there are many features you could easily do without; you could use them as trade-offs to get the ice cream features incorporated.

Sorry, Nell informs you. She's already done the analysis and design and has begun coding. The feature set was locked in when we had those interviews; we can't go back and change them without adding to time and cost. Darn! You now realize you're either not going to have the software in time for the festival or you're going to have to live without the ice cream features, which are critical if you add that to your business. You begin to wish you had never started doing business with Nell.

7.2.2 Disadvantages of Waterfall

Waterfall lifecycles have not worked well in the creation of business software. They have contributed to our pitiful success ratio and much frustration and overtime for technology professionals. The reality of today's business is that things change constantly. In the 1970s business changed, too, but at a slower pace. Corporations could take years to create new products, months to make decisions, and weeks to provide customer service. In the twenty-first century, those time windows have shrunk dramatically. Forget about e-Business as the reason, this is an issue of global competitiveness. Every industry has so many more new players from around the world that customers (businesses and consumers) can expect and demand changes to happen quickly or instantly. Those businesses that can offer the best quality, the lowest price, and the greatest ability to adapt to customer needs consistently win. The business software must accommodate those needs as well. If internal software departments or companies cannot keep up with the rate of change in business, the business world will find some way around them. Nell's insistence on an unchanging set of features for one month might not have seemed unreasonable to Nell, but to the coffee shop owner that was an unworkable assumption. Yet, even he could not tell Nell what changes he expected to make during that month in the interviews with her at the beginning. He couldn't even remember to tell her everything he did know; no one's perfect.

In process terms, we call the waterfall lifecycle "brittle." If nothing changes and no one forgets anything during the lifecycle, waterfall works well. Unfortunately, this rarely, if ever, happens in the creation of business software. Add the fact that the average business software project takes much longer than one month, probably closer to 6–12 months, and you can see the scope of the problem.

This brittleness to changes is interesting. Whenever you speak to someone in the software field, the topic of change comes up often. The change we are mainly concerned about is the rate of change of technology. But the rate of change in business causes us many more problems, especially when we utilize the waterfall lifecycle. Change in business requirements we see mainly as a people problem. If businesspeople were more reasonable, less demanding, knew what they wanted, and could make up their minds, that problem would go away. But masking it as a people problem is not the answer.

There are other issues with waterfall that Nell and the coffee shop owner did not even encounter. Waterfall projects often have a problem with risk. By executing activity-by-activity, we push the risk of the system actually working to specification far into the future, devilishly close to the end of the project. These questions will not be answered until late in the lifecycle:

- Will the businesspeople accept the system?
- Will they enjoy using it?
- Have we represented it accurately with our artifacts (analysis models, user interface storyboards, prototypes, etc.)?
- Will the pieces of technology work together as we've planned?
- Will the team perform the tasks quickly enough to meet the deadline?
- Will the quality be high enough to avoid excessive problems in testing or production?
- Will there be business changes that occur in this lifecycle that make our delivery on-time and on-schedule impossible?

The longer the lifecycle (3/6/9/12/18/24/36 months) the more risk there is.

Table 7.2 Disadvantages of Waterfall

Changes that occur after an activity is complete disrupt the lifecycle. For instance, changes to requirements that are known only after the requirements activity is complete will either (a) increase the cost/effort, (b) lengthen the schedule, or (c) cause user dissatisfaction if not implemented.

High rates of change are the norm, whether in Internet software companies, automotive manufacturers, energy producers, state government, or banks. No area of business is untouched by the "change bug."

The idea of gathering "all the requirements" at an early stage of the lifecycle is made impractical by human nature (forgetting, missing the point) and business changes.

Businesspeople see trade-offs in features as much fair game as trade-offs in schedule, cost, and quality. Waterfall lifecycle managers, however, can only handle schedule and cost, with quality usually being an underdiscussed topic, something that suffers when everything else is held constant. With waterfall, changes in features after the requirements activity cannot happen without cascading changes in schedule and/or cost.

What About Change Management?

You may be thinking that this desecration of waterfall lifecycles sounds like heresy. (But if we were writing a book that just confirmed all your existing beliefs, why read it?)

You may say to yourself, "I have mechanisms for dealing with change throughout the lifecycle; I even have a discipline called 'change management' that covers this need." True. However, we feel that the term *change management* is not representative of the true aim of this activity. Change management sounds like accepting that things will change constantly throughout the lifecycle and you have created a system to handle incorporation of those changes into the end product when they make sense. In every instance we've seen, the actual activity is more aptly called *change discouragement*. Keep changes from disrupting the lifecycle as much as possible. Lock them down. When they are absolutely necessary, use trade-offs in cost, schedule, or quality to offset the required rework for already completed activities as well as additional tasks in upcoming activities. Changes that are possible are those which cause the least disruption of the lifecycle, the least rework of completed activities. If we are right in using this new name, does it give the impression of a software organization committed to changing with the business?

In our software project management, we have the goal of "reducing disruptive change to a minimum." But the businesspeople are looking to us to "handle as much change as possible." Our views are seriously at odds.

7.3 Alternatives to Waterfall

If the waterfall model is in conflict with today's fast-changing business world, what are the alternatives? There have certainly been several models proposed since the introduction of waterfall that help to solve some of these problems.

7.3.1 Rapid Application Development (RAD)

Waterfall lifecycles have increased risk as the schedule of the project lengthens. A methodology called rapid application development (RAD) helped address this by pulling the business users in more tightly into the lifecycle. Sessions called joint application development (JAD) brought all the stakeholders together and basically designed the system as a group. Also, RAD lifecycles relied on prototyping to share information among users and technologists. The feedback loops were tightened using these techniques and tools.

RAD did not work well for several reasons. First, as we examined in Chapter 1, prototypes are not good artifacts for discussion about software requirements. They tend to shift the focus of businesspeople onto the lesser important factors of design (user interface widgets, Web page navigation, and so on) and away from the important requirements. They also often set unrealistic expectations of how far the project has progressed based on "how complete it looks."

Also, although RAD was a step toward adaptivity, it did not have enough specific tools and techniques to deal with a constant flow of changes coming from the business to allow teams to function effectively. As a result, RAD became a satisfactory lifecycle for small projects, but was deemed as insufficient for endeavors with more than three to four member teams operating for 3–4 months or more.

7.3.2 Spiral

The Spiral lifecycle, credited largely to Barry Boehm (1986), uses a series of iterations to refine the understanding of the project scope and reduce the risk. The Spiral lifecycle is effective in peeling away the layers of a large project scope. It relies on prototypes or simulations early in the lifecycle.

The Spiral lifecycle does much to reduce risk in the software lifecycle. However, prototypes and simulations can tend to pull away the attention of a business user to unimportant details instead of important requirements. However, it is accurate to say that the iterative/incremental lifecycles owe much to the Spiral philosophy that preceded them.

For an example of the Spiral process, see this link:

http://metr.cua.edu/faculty/mckenzie/mis327/Spiral.html

7.3.3 Staged Delivery

If larger projects cause bigger risks and problems, why not reduce a large project into smaller subprojects? The Staged Delivery lifecycle has taken hold in the software industry in a big way. A large project, which taken in one big chunk, would take two years and a team of twenty people, can theoretically be broken down into eight smaller pieces, each subproject taking three months and ten people. These individual subprojects are much more manageable, and much less risky.

The difficulties in Staged Delivery are about the "cutting." What are the best dividing lines to cut the project into smaller pieces? If you attack the Forecasting subsystem first, will there be so much dependence on the other subsystems that you'll end up developing the whole application before getting Forecasting to work? Also, new software that is replacing old software is problematic for Staged Delivery. When does the point come where the old system can be turned off? How will the old system accomplish some of the functionality not implemented yet in the new system, but turn off the functionality already done in the new system?

Also, within each "stage" the Staged Delivery lifecycle is still waterfall. This means that, like our friend Nell, even though the projects are short (perhaps 3–6 months) their ability to adapt to business changes during the lifecycle is feeble.

7.3.4 Holistic Iterative/Incremental (HI/I)

Taking much of what works in other lifecycles, a variety of methodologists in the late 1990s put together lifecycles that could be summed up as holistic iterative/incremental (HI/I— pronounced *hi-eye*). Lifecycles such as the Unified Process (UP), eXtreme Programming (XP), Adaptive Software Development (ASD), and Agile Software Development (AgileSD) use tools and techniques that make it possible for a software team to keep up with the massive changes in business today. Although these lifecycles are not specific to business software development (they claim to cover military, real-time, and scientific software as well), they solve the major issues we've faced with waterfall and other earlier lifecycles in the business world.

The HI/I lifecycles have a rigorous focus on continuous feedback loops between software development and its stakeholders, primarily in our case, businesspeople. What differentiates them from RAD, Spiral, or other older lifecycles is that the HI/I lifecycles have a built-in "holistic perspective," in which the view of the whole is never lost. This is accomplished with a strong architectural vision.

7.4 Introducing the Holistic Iterative/Incremental Use-Case-Driven Project Lifecycle

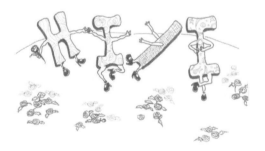

Introducing the Holistic Iterative/Incremental
Lifecycle (HI/I or Hi-Eye)

DEFINITION: The words *iterative* and *incremental* are often, incorrectly, used interchangeably. Understanding each term is important to knowledge of the overall approach.

Iterative means redoing something several times, increasing richness, comprehensiveness, and consistency each time.

Incremental means creating something piece by piece and integrating the pieces into the whole a little at a time.

7.4.1 The Meaning of *Iterative*

Look at the illustration where the totem pole is being constructed iteratively. Notice how the artisan goes through stages of doneness, making each pass a little more detailed and defined. He may have to shave off some carved bits of wood in a later pass. In software development, we call this recoding, or, more accurately, refactoring.

Another metaphor for iterative development might be painting a house. First, you put on a primer coat. This is often a completely different color from the one you are going to use later, maybe beige or white, but it works well for the primer. You just slap it on, not worrying about whether it is perfectly even or whether it looks nice. Then you add the first coat of the finishing paint. This coat is the right color, but it is still a little uneven when you apply it. Perhaps another coat is required to smooth out the color and texture because some parts of the wood soak up more paint than others. In the final iteration, you apply the finishing coat of paint. This paint must be evenly applied and nicely textured. It should look exactly right in all places. It should cover every area of the wall, even the nooks and crannies.

In the context of this book, an iterative approach to requirements specification includes the refinement of use cases and business rules through a series of brushstrokes, which we categorize as Facade, Filled, and Focused iterations.

In *The Unified Software Development Process* (Jacobson 1999), the authors outline several things that iteration is not:

- Random hacking
- A playpen for developers
- Something that affects only developers

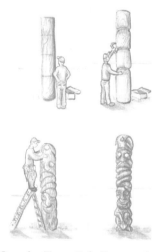

Iterative Totem Pole Construction

- Redesigning the same thing over and over until the developers finally chance on something that works
- Unpredictable
- An excuse for failing to plan and manage

7.4.2 The Meaning of *Incremental*

In incremental development, you create something in small parts. If you were building a house incrementally, you'd build one room at a time. First, you'd put up the bathroom. Then you'd add the kitchen. You'd put a door on this tiny house to keep the elements out. At this point you could begin living in it. Next, you'd add a bedroom. Then a living room. Later, a dining room and extra bedroom. The creation of each room is not willy-nilly—it follows a design—and the benefit is that you can start living in the house a lot sooner than if you waited until the whole house was built. What's more, you will need heating, ventilation, plumbing, and electricity for just the bathroom, the first increment. So you get to try working with these subsystems early in the project, giving yourself an opportunity to evaluate the risks and problems very early. If you find you've used inadequate wiring in the first increment, you need to rip it out of the walls of only one room, a big savings over if you had built the whole house already. With houses, the builders are already quite knowledgeable about the process and constraints, so they tend not to need this incremental approach. But with software, a much less mature industry, we need help from the incremental approach, in every case except where the goal is crystal clear and the environment is exceptionally stable, which doesn't happen often.

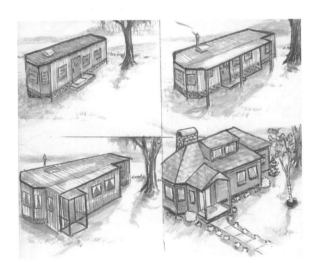

Incremental House Construction

Alistair Cockburn calls this kind of methodology build-deliver-learn. By cutting the application into lots of small chunks of functionality and delivering them separately, you get a chance to learn from your mistakes during the early iterations.

In the context of this book, an incremental approach to requirements specification includes completing batches of use cases and business rules together, but not assuming that all artifacts must be completed at the same time. For instance, of a total of 25 identified use cases, your team may create 5, then proceed through analysis/design/construction/testing/deployment for those 5. While those use cases are being built, part of the team can tackle the next five, and so on.

SEE ALSO: http://members.aol.com/acockburn

7.4.3 The Meaning of *Holistic*

Looking at an iterative/incremental lifecycle, one shortfall tends to be evident. If you are creating software piece-by-piece, and iterating to make it right, how do you keep the big picture in mind? How do you ensure that the pieces work together effectively to solve the overall goal?

These are reasonable questions. A major risk of failure in iterative/incremental projects is the loss of focus on the big picture and an end product that is a mish-mash of pieces that do not operate as a whole.

One side of the solution to this paradox is software architecture. Software architecture (a term borrowed from the building industry) is the underlying structure of a software application. The person in charge of this is the software architect. This role becomes even more crucial in an iterative/incremental project, because now the architecture needs to play the role of keeping these iterations focused on the end goal. In a waterfall project, many architects fell into the role of defining hardware/software standards and then stood aside as the program code was created. No more! An architect is a hands-on manager who ensures that the end product hangs together. Architecture encompasses many aspects: component interfaces, application layers/tiers, deployment environment, security, multiprocessing, data access, configuration management, coding and data communication standards, hardware, and package usage.

A second side of the solution to a holistic iterative/incremental process is business strategy alignment. If software architecture is about staying true to the technological vision of the application, then business strategy alignment is about staying true to the business vision of the application.

Business strategy alignment makes the assumption that a business strategy exists. A strategy is much more than a mission statement. It may consist of mission, vision, values, and a set of high-level steps that will get the business moving toward those goals. Then the individual initiatives undertaken within the organization need to be tied back to the strategy. Usually, some type of framework is required to do this. We use the Purdue Enterprise Reference Architecture (PERA) to accomplish this alignment back to the business strategy.

It is a generic business model that provides alignment of technology initiatives back to the business strategy. If the business strategy is not defined, PERA helps create one. PERA is in the public domain; it is not proprietary to us or any other consulting company.

SEE: http://iies.www.ecn.purdue.edu/IIES/PLAIC/PERA/Publications

7.4.4 The Meaning of *Adaptivity*

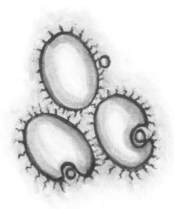

The use case process needs to be as adaptive as a living organism.

The goal of the holistic iterative/incremental lifecycle is to achieve adaptivity. We show our definition of adaptivity here:

adaptivity n. 1. capability of making suitable or fitting a specific situation

Again, two terms are often used interchangeably: adaptivity and adaptability. But adaptability is a different quality:

adaptability n. 1. capability of being made suitable or fitted to a specific situation

Using these definitions, adaptivity is much more dynamic than adaptability. An adaptive system will adapt itself to a new situation. An adaptable system can be changed to suit a new situation, but it will not change itself.

For example, when a business requirement changes, an adaptive software development team is able to take it in stride without missing a beat. An adaptable team can incorporate the changed requirement, but there is disruption and a loss of productivity as the group rethinks its approach.

Of course, the application of these terms is relative. Is any software development team completely adaptive? We've never seen it. However, in comparing a team to the industry, you could see that a particular team can handle changes much more easily and effortlessly than other teams, and therefore judge it to be an adaptive team.

7.4.5 Complex Adaptive Systems

The concept of adaptivity has gained tremendous visibility in the past ten years with the acceleration of research into complex adaptive systems. In the Santa Fe Institute in New Mexico, scientists from many disciplines (economics, physics, biology, chemistry, computer science, and others) came together to begin their study of why complex systems behaved in ways that seemed completely strange and unpredictable (Waldrop 1992). They knew that small changes to a single variable in a complex system could reverberate through the system until it had gone into what appeared to be complete chaos. To sum up their goal, these scientists were determined to make sense of chaos. (Sound like any software projects you've experienced lately?)

As they progressed, they found that complex adaptive systems do, indeed, act in a consistent way. Complex adaptive systems include a pond ecosystem, the human brain and body, city traffic, a business, an airport, an industry, a country, a stock market, and the weather. A description of chaos theory (which ideas preceded complexity) often goes like this: A butterfly flapping its wing in Singapore can create a hurricane in South Carolina. The idea is that small changes of a small number of the input variables into a complex adaptive system can cause very large changes to occur in the system.

Using large computer models to track the changes in the systems when input variables changed, they found that these systems had a center point to which they would return after the reverberations of input changes. They called this center point a "strange attractor." Using this as an anchor for more research, they found that these seemingly "chaotic" systems operate in a consistent, although not predictable, way.

In software, we have begun to realize—after much learning from our mistakes—that our projects and processes are complex adaptive systems. People are unpredictable by definition. Requirements and business priorities change constantly. Technology is like a treadmill moving and changing and improving. These factors contribute to a very dynamic environment, one that resembles a living organism much more than a machine (Highsmith 2000). This means we need to be focused on making our processes adaptive instead of optimizing, which is our current focus. Tools and models like the Capability Maturity Model (CMM) and its derivatives, ISO 9000 quality certification and others, focus on optimizing an organization to produce as much as possible with as few resources as possible. This works for an organization where change is not an issue; however, most of our organizations have constant change as a very prominent issue. For us, adaptivity is the key.

Listen for the metaphors that are used on your projects. If you regularly hear the following metaphors, you can be pretty sure the team thinks of itself as a machine:

- "We need to work together like cogs in a wheel."
- "This team is running like a top."
- "The squeaky wheel gets the oil."
- "Those businesspeople are always changing their minds."
- "We are a lean, mean programming machine!"

- "Let's crank out that code."
- "We will let this project go for another month before we turn it off."
- "He really threw a wrench/spanner in the works when he added that requirement."

On the other hand, if these are the metaphors you hear, your team thinks of itself as a living organism, adaptive to change:

- "Let's see where this takes us."
- "It's okay, we can change right along with the business."
- "This product has grown into something good."
- "Let's breathe life into this product."
- "This product will evolve into something more comprehensive in the next release."

The project that most resembles a living organism is the project that will effectively keep up with the business. The project that resembles a machine will break down and cause problems in any business situation that is fast-changing, dynamic, and unpredictable. Your goal is to move your corner of the world toward becoming a living organism. But how?

7.5 Process

In this section, we'll provide the details of the "how" for holistic iterative/incremental. Although our book is focused on creating good quality requirements for software products, we feel it is necessary to show how those requirements can effectively drive an HI/I lifecycle.

From a software process perspective, we've been sleeping while our businesspeople have been changing dramatically. The world of business in North America, and indeed around the world, has changed incredibly since the 1970s:

- Globalization of markets has increased competition and trade.
- Time-to-market has become a huge competitive advantage once cost and quality of products and services are equal (which is more likely to happen in a global economy).
- Price pressure keeps increasing, causing businesspeople to constantly re-examine what they can remove of their own costs.
- Business books of the last few decades have had titles like:
  - *The Living Organization* (Guillory 2000)
  - *Thriving on Chaos* (Peters 1991)
  - *Leadership and the New Science, Second Edition* (Wheatley 2001)
  - *Birth of the Chaordic Age* (Hock 2000)
  - *Adaptive Enterprise* (Haeckel 1999)

These are not new concepts in business. Some of these books are over 20 years old. Businesses have been borrowing from complexity science for some time now, to help them adapt to globalization and other complex environmental factors. In software, however, we seem to be clinging to the thought that we can stay "organized" while business is flying around in its chaordic state. (*Chaordic* is a state of being at the edge of chaos and order.)

Yes, we're aware that several methodologies have arrived that tout the adaptive lifecycle. The RUP is the most popular, providing a highly detailed methodology centered on the iterative/incremental concept. XP is a set of process patterns that give advice as to how software could be created using iterative/incremental techniques. It is not meant to be a methodology; it does not describe a lifecycle nor does it provide artifact definitions. However, it is often thought of as a competitor to RUP, in that both describe an iterative/incremental way of developing software. (eXtreme Programming has no link whatever to Microsoft's Windows XP "eXPerience" operating system.)

What is interesting is that, although many organizations have purchased the books, CDs, and training for these methodologies, hardly any have actually "converted" to an iterative/incremental process. Organizations, including in-house shops and especially consulting firms, have merely relabeled their deliverable names, with requirements specification becoming use cases, dataflow diagrams becoming object model, and project plan becoming iteration plan, without really making the jump to iterative/incremental.

Here are some iterative/incremental myths commonplace in those organizations that we would like to dispel:

Iterations can be any length. Iteration length is extremely important. This is mostly due to human nature. Iteration length is best optimized to the length of time a person can effectively focus on a deadline and a set of functionality without losing concentration. Unfortunately for us humans, this is a very short time, only about 1–3 weeks. Any longer than that, and we lose focus. Also, the focus issue is important with our business sponsors. How long are they willing to wait in their chaordic world before they want to see tangible progress? We're not talking about a release of the product into production necessarily, necessarily, just something that can answer the businessperson's query, "Let's see what you've done so far." And folks, showing them a stack of design documentation will not appease them. It must be running, working code, every 1–3 weeks.

Iterative/incremental is just lots of small waterfalls. This is not entirely false, but it is a bit misrepresentative. The nature of a waterfall lifecycle changes when it is reduced down from 6–9–12 months to only 1–3 weeks. Things become much less formal. The procedures that seemed so important become less so in a more narrowly focused iteration. The best way to find out which procedures are important and which ones haven't been helping is to try a small iteration with a small team and see what you can leave out.

Iterative/incremental can be managed the same way we managed waterfall—task-by-task. This is dead wrong, and you'll die trying. Waterfall projects can be managed by task assignment, because we have (in theory) a situation with little change, and we can plan our tasks assignments far out into the future. Iterative/incremental assumes a dramatic amount of change, and therefore the project managers manage more to the set of requirements than to the set of tasks. Project managers divide the work according to the requirements (use cases), and then the team makes sure that those requirements get implemented in the iteration. Self-managed teams, as far as task assignments go, only work on a small scale. So, the idea of iterative/incremental is that, if you break up that large software application into many small pieces, each of which can be accomplished by a team of three to four people in 1–3 weeks, your project managers can worry less about tasks and more about the series of requirements to implement.

We can still test manually. Again, by breaking up our project schedule into many mini-implementations (iterations), we change the nature of the lifecycle. When we test the first iteration of code, we test all the functionality the team built that week (or 2–3 weeks). In the second iteration, we test iterations one plus two. Imagine the testing effort in iteration fifteen. Automated test tools are a must. Regression testing tools will test application functionality (Mercury Interactive WinRunner, Segue SilkTest, Rational Robot, and so on), and load/stress testing tools will test the architectural soundness of the application (Mercury Interactive LoadRunner, Segue SilkPerformer, Rational TeamTest, and so on).

We must keep our team from having to redo work. The impulse to keep teams from "rework" is a holdover from basing our software projects on industrial-age projects, such as building a bridge or creating a factory. Rework is essential to a business software project. Avoiding rework is part of "optimization." Projects that hold an optimization focus are those where the goal is well understood at the beginning of the lifecycle and changes are rare during the lifecycle. The opposite focus of optimizing is adaptivity. Adaptivity means that the team is trying different approaches, cutting its losses on things that don't work, and charging forward when something does work.

We need to deploy every iteration of code. This will be hard to do, and a bit wasteful in the early iterations. Most teams will need to postpone true deployment onto the target hardware/software/database environment until a few iterations have been created and it is worth undergoing the overhead of deployment.

7.6 Principles of the Holistic Iterative/Incremental Software Lifecycle

The HI/I lifecycle is guided by a set of general principles. In this section, we'll look at each principle and explain how it relates to the goal of effective management.

- Manage requirements not tasks.
- The important goals are the business goals—dates and budgets.
- Think like a businessperson—What have you done for me lately?
- Divide and conquer.
- Cut the job into programs and projects (cut at the thinnest part).
- Tie everything back to the business.
- Create demonstrable deliverables.
- Learn the art of "good enough" quality.
- The pieces will be smaller than you think.
- Expect negotiation, not specification.
- Forget about baselines, sign-offs.

- Estimate by doing.
- Calculate return-on-investment in a new way using portfolios.

7.6.1 Manage Requirements Not Tasks

In a HI/I lifecycle, project managers are far more aware of the requirements of the project than we would be in a waterfall lifecycle. This is because the requirements are the building blocks for project scheduling and team assignments. For instance, in a waterfall world, a project manager might give a team the responsibility to "design the credit rating calculation component." This is a specific set of tasks that relate to design, not analysis, not coding, not testing, and so on. It is also scoped by stating that the team should attack only the credit rating calculation part of the business problem, not customer service, not interest rate calculation, not monthly statementing, and so on.

However, the interfaces between this activity and other activities are huge. Being designers, they will need to find out what requirements and analysis were done and understand that effort fully. Maybe they did those tasks, maybe they didn't. Then they will need to formulate the results of their design efforts in a way that will be easily understood by the development, testing, and deployment teams coming later. There are many, many, many interfaces between teams in this scenario. Not to mention the interfaces between credit rating calculation and the other business functions.

In a HI/I lifecycle, the assignment is quite different. A team will be assigned responsibility for implementing a specific set of requirements. Using the process we've described in this book, the team may be assigned implementation responsibility for a set of use case paths or nonfunctional requirements. For instance, the team may be assigned implementation responsibility for the use case path "Enter New Credit Card Customer—basic path." The team will need to make sure the pieces are in place to make that functionality demonstrable by the end of the iteration. When they are done with the iteration, someone should be able to sit down at the computer and go through all the steps that are specified in the use case "Enter New Credit Card Customer" in the basic path. The user interface might not be very jazzy, error processing might not be working (that will come when we do exception paths), but the whole process is possible to complete from a businessperson's perspective.

This type of planning is very different from waterfall task assignment. But the advantages are many:

- The businessperson can see tangible progress at the end of each quick iteration (1–3 weeks).
- The team has the ability to adapt when changes occur, even in the middle of the iteration, because the design has not already been set in stone.
- The team's motivation level starts and remains high because they are producing tangible results regularly, giving the "instant gratification" that so many people crave.
- The interfaces between teams are fewer than with waterfall task assignment. The team accomplishing this use case interfaces mainly with the architecture team, who

ensures that the team's work fits into the overall technical structure, and with the business analysts, who ensure that the team's work fits in with the business goals.

- The team is composed of a cross-functional set of individual contributors: presentation designer/coders, business layer designer/coders, data access designer/coders, data modelers/database administrators, and other technical specialists. This helps create less animosity between disciplines (the testing group dislikes the development group, for example) because the project teams are judged on their success together, not as functional silos. Also, it allows for more variation of methods and practices, so experimentation can bring new ways of making the product better quality or produced more quickly.

7.6.2 The Important Goals Are the Business Goals— Dates and Budgets

If you live in a community where a stadium has recently been built, think back to that lifecycle. The pronouncement came that the city would build a grand monument to itself, which would attract professional sports teams, circuses, and other incredible events. Various contractors got involved to create the stadium concept, an interesting architectural design, and a set of cost estimates. The project proceeded and finally was usable.

What do you remember from the stadium construction? Over budget?
Behind schedule? Or on-time, within budget, with a few things undone?

What do you remember from the stadium lifecycle? If the stadium went over budget, you heard about it. The newspapers reported it, especially if the taxpayers bore the cost of the overrun, which is often the case. Also, if the stadium was late in coming to completion, everyone remembers that too. If the stadium was over budget or behind schedule, we noticed.

What is interesting is what we do not remember about the stadium. If a stadium was within budget and within schedule, but still had some components not operational at the time of "completion," did anyone talk about it? Let's say the stadium was declared complete, but several of the "nosebleed sections" did not have chairs put in yet. Did anyone care? Or, more accurately, did anyone care as much about that as they did about schedule and budget?

What was your role in the stadium lifecycle? You were probably a "user" if you were interested in using the stadium after it was built and also a "stakeholder" if you were paying the taxes to get it built.

Now, take that mind-set to the software projects you've been involved in. Which projects do you consider successes and which ones failures? Examine your own viewpoints here versus the stadium and see what is different.

In the software world, we have based our scoping restrictions on the feature set of the applications, rather than the schedule and budget. Get those requirements nailed down early, we think, and you'll have success. By defining the set of requirements early and then trying to discourage any changes to them throughout the lifecycle, we may be missing the business point. The requirements set should always be the most flexible in changes, while schedule and budget must be the least flexible. With the waterfall lifecycle, we've got it backwards, think our businesspeople. They're right!

7.6.3 Think Like a Businessperson—What Have You Done for Me Lately?

A complaint that businesspeople often make is that the stock market has a short memory and little foresight. The focus is on today. Or, at best, "What have you done for me lately?" In fact, this is a reality of business, whether it is a public company or not. Business is unforgiving and temporal. Businesspeople are the same way, if they are successful. Most businesses are evaluated, internally and externally, by fiscal quarter (three months). Financial results are reported to the stakeholders and problems are discussed. Investments are evaluated for their contributions to revenue and profits.

Have you ever been on a software project that was cancelled? It may have been cancelled for "budget reasons." The executives were doing their quarterly evaluation of their investments, including the money they were pouring into your project, and they decided it was no longer worth it. "Cut our losses." Unfair? Probably. Why did it happen?

Projects that create results that tangibly help the business increase revenue, increase profit, or decrease costs are projects that are less likely to get cancelled. And how often do those results need to be created? At least quarterly. If your project has gone for more than three months without producing a result that helps the business, it is at risk. Right now, businesspeople are looking at that outflow of money, seeing no return yet and asking that question, "What have you done for me lately?"

7.6.4 Divide and Conquer

Of course, a project manager needs to take a large endeavor and break it up into smaller pieces. This is a fundamental task of project management. Work breakdown structure, task definition, and assignment, resource allocation—this activity goes by many names. Essentially, there is a lot of work to do. The project manager needs to take that work and divide it up among a team of people to get it done.

The most important part of this activity is—where to cut? What is the most effective way to carve up the big chunk of work and allocate it to teams who have different skills, skill levels, specializations, career paths, and tools? There are several common ways of allocation.

One is by technology. Certain people have certain technical skills, so you give them the work that matches what they are good at. For instance, one team may be responsible for presentation (user interface, Web pages, navigation, screen widgets, and so on). Another team may take the business rules layer (creation of the business objects, controllers, and so on). A third team may take the data mapping layer (moving data back and forth between the business rules layer and the relational database). A fourth team may test; a fifth team may create the database; a sixth may handle architecture, and so on. Each of these layers requires specific technical skills and experience with the architecture to get the work done efficiently.

Another is by subsystem. Business applications can typically be broken up into subsystems, handling work done by different business departments. In a human resources management system, the subsystems may be payroll, benefits, career planning, recruiting, and company social activities. Each of those subsystems could be assigned to a team who builds the components to handle that business function.

A third is by requirement (use case). The teams are assigned sets of use cases and they are responsible for creating working software that makes those use cases possible.

Edward de Bono (de Bono 1994) has a creativity tool called PMI—plus, minus, interesting. We'll use that tool here to compare these three methods of dividing and conquering.

7.6.4.1 Dividing and Conquering by Technology
Plus

- Teams are composed of like-skilled members who may systematize their technical disciplines and advance their approaches together (for example, testers together in a group may create a testing methodology).
- When you create a process where the baton moves from technical group to group, it is easy to see what the status is (for example, the process moves from the business analysts to systems analysts to developers to testers, and so on).

Minus

- Each group starts to see the other groups as their enemies (for example, those developers are always passing the code to us testers too late for us to do our job).
- Dividing by technology tends to reinforce the waterfall lifecycle (for minuses of waterfall, see Table 7.2).
- The interfaces between the groups are not clean. All groups need to pass a tremendous amount of information back and forth, especially if an iterative process is used (for example, groups will be attending each other's meetings, need to know each other's processes, and so on).

Interesting

What happens when technology changes dramatically for one group that has an effect on another group?

7.6.4.2 Dividing and Conquering by Subsystem

Plus

- This approach gives the team more appreciation for the business problems being solved, as each group specializes in part of the business.
- The technical groups tend to form better relationships with the SMEs in the business groups.

Minus

Business subsystems are often harder to determine than at first glance. If they are divided by business department, often there are situations where several departments need to use the same functions, so it becomes unclear which subsystem group should take responsibility. Also, with workflows, it becomes unclear where along the workflow one subsystem stops and the next one takes over.

Interesting

What happens when the departments are reorganized or reengineered? Will the system still function in a sensible way for the business?

7.6.4.3 Dividing and Conquering by Use Case

Plus

- Each piece, when developed, can be tested and demonstrated to the businesspeople as a coherent bit of functionality that accomplishes a business goal.
- Use cases are more fine-grained than subsystems or technology, so the smaller use case work packages can be shuffled around as teams need more or less work throughout the lifecycle.
- Each use case goes end-to-end, through presentation-business rules-data mapping-database-architecture, so everything can be integrated and tested early and often.
- Since the teams to accomplish one use case must be interdisciplinary, the teams become more cohesive and less likely to build walls between technical specialties (presentation, database admin, and so on).

Minus

- Project managers, who have been occupied with task tracking, now must understand the use cases and they will have to spend more time learning about the requirements.
- Can lead to a functionality-centric viewpoint, where nonfunctional requirements and systemwide architecture get ignored.

- If the architecture group is not strong, the use cases may be too independent of each other, where common components are developed multiple times and common patterns and metaphors are not followed.

Interesting

Will teams who are new to use cases be able to divide and conquer this way?

Because of the issues that occur with the other methods, we strongly recommend dividing and conquering by use cases. It results in better products, earlier results, more cohesive teams, and better architecture.

7.6.5 Cut the Job into Programs and Projects

In many software organizations, new groups have sprung up called Program Management Offices (PMOs). The idea of these groups is to centralize people who have the skill to manage large projects, a very rare skill indeed. Few jobs are as stressful or demanding as the job of a program/project manager.

It is worth defining the difference between project and program.

- A project is an undertaking requiring concerted effort.
- A program is a set of projects that benefit from being managed together.

A project manager takes responsibility for the execution of the "undertaking." He tracks the progress and handles the problems that arise. Our friend Jeff Jamison, a great project manager, says that the project manager's job is to "be further up the road from his team, clearing roadblocks and plugging potholes." He's right. The project manager has a vision of the upcoming weeks and months and is making sure that things fit together as the team progresses toward its goals and deadlines.

A program manager has a slightly different role. Since a program manager is responsible for multiple projects, she will be in contact with multiple project managers. Program managers are concerned with the interconnections between those projects: interdependent deadlines, functionality linkage, staffing swaps, requirements overlaps, and so on.

Program managers also get involved in reporting on the combined status of the multiple projects, including budgeting.

The role of the program manager versus the project team is illustrated with a metaphor provided to us by Jim Hendrickson, a friend, project manager, visionary, songwriter, and United States veteran:

Imagine that the project is a jet fighter that needs to land on an aircraft carrier in the South Pacific. The roles are

- Project manager (jet pilot)
- Program manager (air traffic controller on the aircraft carrier)

When the plane is farther than 50 miles away from the aircraft carrier, the pilot has a lot of freedom. He can fly around, do flips, do whatever.

Jet Landing on an Aircraft Carrier

Once he gets within 50 miles of the aircraft carrier, he must begin communicating to the air traffic controller (ATC). They negotiate the terms of the landing. The ATC instructs the pilot of his vicinity to other planes, as well as the need to fit in with other planes landing soon. The ATC also requires that the pilot decide on one of several available approach patterns. The pilot chooses an approach and continues moving toward the aircraft carrier.

As the jet gets closer to the aircraft carrier, the communication between the pilot and the ATC becomes more intense. The pilot is constantly stating his perspective: the readings from the gauges in the plane, his view through his windows, his requirements. The ATC is also giving her perspective: other planes that have landed and are moving out of the way, weather conditions, radar readings of other aircraft in the area.

During landing, the communication must be flawless—back-and-forth messages about both perspectives, move up a little, your left wing is too low, and so on.

The communication starts fairly casually, gets more intense, and becomes ultimately meticulous and thorough through landing.

Note that the pilot (project manager) is at the controls of the jet throughout. At no time does the ATC (program manager) say "you're not doing well enough landing this plane, we're taking over." What a disaster that would be. Probably possible with wireless remote computer control, but not desirable by anyone. The same should be true of the relationship between program and project managers.

We have held back from saying that project managers "report to" program managers. We don't think that is exactly true. The program managers provide a service to project managers, but the project managers need to be ultimately in charge of "landing the plane."

Also, you'll notice something interesting with Jim's metaphor. The amount of communication starts small, then increases to a frenzy by the time landing (implementation) occurs. This is how the relationship should work on software projects too. Program managers need to give the projects a lot of latitude at the beginning of the project, but inch down on the specifics further and further as the team approaches implementation. This doesn't mean lazy or slack communications—they still need to be precise—but there can be less communication at the beginning than later on.

The Project Management Institute (PMI)

The Project Management Institute (PMI) provides a tremendous amount of literature, guidance, and training for project and program managers. They offer certification for a manager to become a Project Management Professional (PMP), moving the profession of project management a little closer to the professions of accounting, law, medicine, and so on. Being a true project management professional requires a tremendous amount of skill, a lot of courage, and excellent people skills, especially communication. PMI training for software development managers still focuses mainly on the waterfall lifecycle, but they are moving to correct that issue. (Web site: www.pmi.org)

Program management is a difficult concept to implement well. Certainly, you have heard of the Program Management Office (PMO), a group created to manage multiple projects in an efficient, effective manner. It is very hard to get PMO right, from what we've seen with our clients. The PMO can rapidly deteriorate into a glorified status reporting organization that does not provide much value to the project managers/pilots. Or the program manager can become a type of super-project manager, who manages the managers below him the way a project manager manages the individual project. This is not the intent of setting up programs, nor is it anything more than an annoyance for the project managers. Program managers must keep the role of the air traffic controller in mind with their projects.

Also, in a use case driven lifecycle, where divide and conquer by use case is used, there is another interesting wrinkle. Project managers manage more by requirement, less by task. This is a major change from waterfall project management. The tasks are driven from the use cases the team tackles. The project manager is more interested in "which use cases the team is working on" than the individual tasks people are accomplishing. This can allow the team to self-manage to the point that they can still accomplish the use case functionality in the time allowed.

How to Slice a Use Case

Is it really always that simple? No, never. Here are the issues that arise. Use cases usually contain too much functionality for a team of three or four people to accomplish in a week or two, especially considering they are creating so many components in various areas of technical environment, program design, program code, testing, and deployment. Use cases themselves need to be sliced.

Use cases can be sliced several ways, all desirable in various situations. A use case contains sets of paths, alternative and exception paths. The team can tackle the basic course of events first, then other paths later. This is a very common way

continued

How to Slice a Use Case (continued)

to slice a use case. Alternative paths may be done separately, or grouped together when it makes sense. Exception paths are often grouped together, and are usually done after the basic course of events and most alternative paths are complete.

Another way to slice is to use "roughed-in" components. Let's say the Select Agent use case is undertaken early in the lifecycle, before any real work on the user interface design, including metaphor, widgets, standards, and color themes is ready. The Select Agent team may decide to "rough in" their user interface very simply, knowing that they will have to replace it later with the real thing. But at least they can get an end-to-end Select Agent use case working, with a visual (if not particularly appealing) user interface for the businesspeople to play with. Other components can be roughed in too: dummy database tables, software objects (interfaces defined but only roughed in for method implementation), package calls (dummy interfaces), and so on.

The team will create the user interface, the business rules layer, data mapping, and database tables to make the use case work.

7.6.6 Tie Everything Back to the Business

Project managers who must manage every task and every assignment may not be able to tie those tasks specifically back to the original business needs. However, if project managers become focused on management by use cases, they can have a clearer traceability of the tasks back to the business requirements because the use cases *are* the business requirements.

Further, once a team has completed an iteration making a use case "real," the businesspeople can inspect the use case and make sure it accurately reflects what they need. In fact, "what they need" may even have changed slightly (or drastically!) between the time they provided those specifications and now. This gives them a chance to fold in any new requirements, which can be addressed in the upcoming iterations.

A businessperson will be much more comfortable seeing a project schedule that maps out when each piece of functionality (use case, non-functional) will be complete, rather than a task-oriented schedule (divided by technology or subsystem). Plus, he gets the chance to provide input regularly by playing with the real system, as it is built.

The value of this short feedback loop cannot be overstated. It is a tremendous way to stay on target, even when that target is moving. (Do they ever stay still?) Short feedback loops are the only way to stay on track in today's crazy world of business and technology.

Why not use a prototype? There are several reasons. First, businesspeople need to interact with the real system. If they comment on some specific need for change and the team responds, "well, the real system will act differently," then the feedback path is lost.

Second, remember the prototyping efforts you've been involved in. How many people were dedicated to maintaining the prototype? How much fun was it making sure that the prototype reflected the real system, and the real system was incorporating the changes in the prototype that were requested by the businesspeople? Not much. Allow the businesspeople access to the real system, and let the real system evolve under their fingertips.

7.6.7 Create Demonstrable Deliverables

This lifecycle of creating a feedback loop between the businesspeople and the real system is called creating "demonstrable deliverables." Businesspeople do not care about design documents. They do not care about paper or pictorial specifications. They care only about the end result. Does that mean you should forget about analysis and design? Certainly not. It means that when you want to show the businesspeople something, show them the working application. The running, tested code. Nothing less. Not prototypes, not screen snapshots. The only exception to this rule is that user interface storyboards can make sense early in the lifecycle before the first iterations have begun. But those storyboards should be created only after the use cases are far enough along that the businesspeople will not get confused by the user interface details introduced on the storyboards.

7.6.8 Learn the Art of "Good Enough" Quality

Microsoft knows how to build its products to a "good enough" quality level. The rest of us could learn from this.

There is something about Microsoft that is larger than life. Bill Gates is the richest person in the world. Microsoft is the largest and most successful software company in the world. The Windows operating system is installed on over 90% of all personal computers in the world.

Yet the quality of their software is quite poor. Yes, it is complex, but is that really an excuse for the number of crashes we all regularly experience using Microsoft products? There is a joke that if Microsoft built cars, we would all be crashing all the time, even if there were no other cars around.

Microsoft learned the rule of "good enough." While other software companies actually created better quality software, Microsoft learned that success depended on a combination of good enough quality and fast enough time-to-market.

This is a very painful lesson for software engineers. We have always been taught that creating error-free software is the ultimate goal. The closer we can get to that goal, the better. Deadlines, cantankerous users, moving requirements targets—these are the enemy of error-free software.

As sacrilegious as it sounds, we have to shake this mind-set, especially in the HI/I lifecycle. The business does not want error-free software, no matter what they tell you. They are not willing to pay for it. They understand that, as we approach error-free software, the cost increases until, to get those last few bugs out, we approach infinite cost.

7.6.9 The Pieces Will Be Smaller Than You Think

Project managers used to dealing with large technology components or business subsystems as planning elements will be uncomfortable with use cases being much finer grained.

This fine-grained nature is actually a plus for planning. Project managers must resist the urge to "bundle" use cases together in order to assign them to teams.

7.6.10 Expect Negotiation, Not Specification

If asked, a businessperson will say that the number one skill in business is negotiation. Business cannot function without negotiation, and the better you are, the better you'll do in business. However, in the realm of business analysts, project managers, and technology specialists, negotiation is underemphasized. As a result, every interaction between businesspeople and software project team members is a mismatch! Excellent negotiators against people who don't even think it's part of their jobs!

Our advice here has two parts. First—take a negotiation course! You'll need it if you plan to be an effective business analyst, project manager, or any other role that interacts with businesspeople. Second—expect negotiation, not specification, from businesspeople. They come to each meeting expecting to negotiate. If the businesspeople state that some feature "absolutely must be in Release One!" that is most likely a negotiating ploy. Learn how to negotiate. In a HI/I lifecycle, you have the ability to trade requirements in and out of scope later in the lifecycle than with waterfall. Take advantage of that flexibility. The thing we hate to see is a dejected business analyst or project manager coming back from a meeting with the businesspeople saying ,"Well, guess what they just added to the scope?" If they add something, ask them what they are going to remove. As we mentioned about HI/I, negotiate requirements out as your first tactic, and only when that fails, should you negotiate end dates and team size and development costs. It is much better to swap out requirements than to push out the delivery dates and demotivate the team.

7.6.11 Forget about Baselines and Sign-offs

Truces are needed between enemies, not partners.

—KULAK AND GUINEY

Project baselines, like those produced in tools like Microsoft Project or Primavera, are not useful in a HI/I project. Since requirements are trading in and out of scope well into the project time line (perhaps as late as 70% of the way through!) the baselines built on certain tasks being in certain spots in the lifecycle become outdated quickly. Although a project management tool can be useful, baselining is not.

Sign-offs are a relic of waterfall projects. A HI/I lifecycle creates a tight feedback loop between the businesspeople and the software project team. It pulls their interest and participation fully into the project. The system becomes as much their system as the project team's system. Take advantage of that fact and remove the sign-off process completely. Sign-offs will only drive stakes into the ground to highlight the differences between the two sides.

7.6.12 Estimate by Doing

In a HI/I lifecycle, the estimates are refined after each iteration. The estimate at the beginning of the first iteration tackles iterations 1, 2, and maybe 3, but no further (depending on iteration length). Once the first iteration is complete, the estimates for 2 through 4 will be clearer. Iteration 2 will be crystal clear, 3 a little less clear, and 4 just about in focus. Continue this, learn as you progress, and re-estimate after every iteration.

How does this work for fixed-price, outsourced projects? It doesn't, quite frankly! We will define a typical fixed-price project as a project that has fixed cost, schedule, and requirements from the very beginning. An outsourced project is one where the software lifecycle is performed primarily by a third-party software consulting company.

If you have ever been on a well-run fixed price, outsourced project, call us. We haven't had that experience. These projects are extremely problematic, antagonistic between client and contractor, and almost always a disaster for all parties involved. We are not sorry to drive another stake into the heart of the fixed-price project. Software projects are complex enough that they must be partnerships between a client and a contractor, with an agreement that requirements will change throughout, even though the budget and schedule might be limited for business reasons. To fix all three is insanity. But you knew that, didn't you?

As far as outsourced software development, our opinion is that third-party consultants must be used to coach, train, and mentor internal IT department employees, not to do the work themselves. So many times we've seen consultants sweep in to develop a new application and then leave, with the internal staff unaware of how the application works and how to maintain it. The one exception to this rule would be if the client company is too small to have its own IT department, in which case they should likely be looking at packaged solutions instead of custom software.

7.6.13 Calculate Return-on-Investment in a New Way Using Portfolios

Return-on-investment (ROI) is an important factor for another software project. How do you calculate it? There are several factors to evaluate:

- Time saved by the manual processes automated
- Time saved by faster processing using software
- Competitive advantage gained by managing complexity better through software

However, there are lots of intangibles that are hard to measure. If the new application replaces an old one, how can you measure something like better usability? Measuring every mouse movement and keystroke is possible but unlikely to be accurate.

Other applications offer indirect ROI. An application allowing a network security administrator to protect against hacker attacks has ROI, but how would you measure it? The projected cost of a hacker attack, the likelihood of the attack, versus the cost of the software? This would be a difficult task at best.

A new method of ROI calculation has arrived called *portfolio management*. It allows ROI to be viewed as the extent to which risk was mitigated for the enterprise. For extensive information on portfolio management, see *The Real Options Solution—Finding Total Value in a High-Risk World* (Boer 2002) and the article at http://www.portfoliomgt.org/read.asp?ItemID=1222.

8

Requirements Traceability

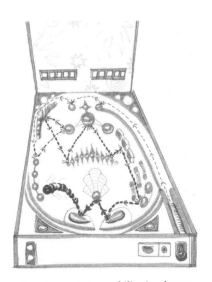

*Requirements traceability is a key to
successful software development.*

NOTE: This chapter assumes some knowledge of an object-oriented software development process, such as the RUP, Object Modeling Technique (OMT), or something similar.

149

One reason for the success of use cases in requirements is effective *traceability*. We define the term as follows:

> *traceability*: clarity of linkage between artifacts

Use cases, when used in the context of a good software lifecycle, can be a tremendous tool for traceability. But first we need to examine what is good about traceability, and, to be fair, the trouble traceability can cause.

Traceability provides assurance that the software at the end of a lifecycle matches what the stakeholders stated they wanted.

Traceability is important because

- Everyone wants to feel like they are building the thing that is supposed to be built.
- Businesspeople often demand to see that the team is doing the provably right thing.
- Large money investments in software mean that we should be able to prove that we are working on the thing we said we would.

When you think about project status in waterfall—we're 60% through development—it shows that we are doing something, but not that we're doing the right thing.

When changes occur, we can see the impact of them rippling through the lifecycle artifacts, which can (a) help business stakeholders to understand the costs of a change and (b) help a team to identify and change all related artifacts for a change.

When stakeholders are viewing system functions later in the lifecycle and see features that they did not expect, traceability can help identify the decision-making process that brought those features in, reducing finger-pointing.

Traceability is hard because

- Stakeholders need change during the lifecycle.
- Team members change.
- A delivery cycle is too long, and it gets off track.
- Things are passed from team to team (designers to developers, and so on) as documents, not hands-on knowledge (throwing over the wall).
- Linkage is not easy between artifact types (contract-style requirements to analysis/design artifacts).

Traceability can create these problems if we're not careful:

- Too many artifacts
- Too many tools with too many integrations
- Too many special "gatekeeper" roles

Traceability is helped by

- Use cases
- Nonfunctionals
- Short feedback loops between the team and the business stakeholders

- Demonstrable inch pebbles
- Daily standups
- Integrations between tools
- Reverse engineering (code to analysis and design, test to requirements, and so on)
- Configuration management
- Collaborative software
- Egalitarianism
- Distributed control

The more egalitarian the collaboration software (and setup) the better. It will be messy and get annoying at times, but the centrally controlled alternative is not acceptable.

Tools that are useful for traceability include

- Documentum eRoom
- Lotus Notes
- Microsoft Exchange
- Intranets
- Groove Networks Groove Workspace
- Bulletin boards
- Newsgroups
- Team member blogs

Automated software lifecycle tools (especially if integrated) include

- Rational Suite
  - Rational RequisitePro
  - Rational Rose
  - Rational XDE
  - Rational ClearCase
  - Rational ClearQuest
  - Rational SQA Robot
  - Rational SQA TeamTest
  - Borland CaliberRM
  - Borland StarTeam
  - Mercury TestDirector
  - Borland TogetherSoft
  - Borland JBuilder
  - Borland CaliberTest
- eXpressroom
- Borland CodeWright
- CompuWare
  - Reconcile
  - QA Partner

8.1 Tracing Back to Use Cases

Use cases are a central traceability artifact in the software lifecycle. What makes them good for traceability is

- They are readable by businesspeople, so they are a credible starting point.
- They are coarse-grained, allowing a large system to be divided up into a digestible number of pieces.

Use case traceability can be extensive, as we've seen on projects we've been a part of. Here are the artifacts use cases can have traceable links:

- Analysis model
- Sequence diagrams
- Class diagrams
- State diagrams
- Design model
- Sequence diagrams
- Class diagrams
- State diagrams
- CRC sessions
- Test model
- Test plans
- Test scenarios
- Test cases
- User interface design
- Storyboards
- Application architecture
- Transaction handling
- Prefetch
- Project management
- Iteration planning
- Documentation and training
- User manual
- User training
- Product marketing
- Security profiles
- Release planning

8.1.1 Analysis Model Traceability

REFERENCE: RUP (analysis model artifact)

The most obvious traceability for any requirements artifact is into analysis. Use cases trace easily into analysis artifacts, especially when the analysis is done using object-oriented techniques.

Using object-oriented analysis as an example, each step in the use case translates into a set of messages passed between objects in a UML sequence diagram. The initiating actor stands on the left of the sequence diagram (as an object in its own right) and initiates the message into the "internal" objects that comprise the application. Analysts create sequence diagrams for each path in each use case.

NOTE: In UML, the *collaboration* diagram is a direct substitute for a *sequence* diagram. Everything we've said about sequence diagrams applies directly to collaboration diagrams. In our experience, we've seen sequence diagrams applied to business problems more than 80% of the time, but the choice is really the preference of the project team and its stakeholders.

An object-oriented analysis model usually also contains a class diagram. The class names come from mining the *nouns* in the use case text. All nouns in the use case names, descriptions, paths, preconditions, and postconditions become candidate classes. Once you collect these nouns, a process of removing class names that are redundant, irrelevant, and attributes of other classes can proceed.

State diagrams are normally part of an object-oriented analysis model. Each state diagram takes one of the classes from the class diagram that exhibits "interesting dynamic behavior" and models the states that this class goes through in its lifetime. A state diagram contains *states* (as you might expect) and *transitions*. The states can often come from the preconditions and postconditions of use cases (although there may be other sources). The transitions are sometimes the messages that come from the initiating actors in the use cases, and other times are the messages from the sequence diagrams.

8.1.2 Design Model Traceability

REFERENCE: RUP (design model artifact)

Design models contain the same artifacts as analysis models: sequence diagrams, class diagrams, and state diagrams. Design models differ in that they contain *boundary* and *control* classes, whereas the analysis models contain only *entity* classes. The control classes are often named directly after the use cases they represent. The boundary classes are a result of the user interface design, so they are only indirectly traceable to use cases.

8.1.3 CRC Card Session Traceability

REFERENCE: CRC card book

CRC (class-responsibility-collaboration) card sessions are an effective tool to determine the operations of classes, also termed responsibility.

In CRC card sessions, the participants hold small recipe cards which have a candidate class name written at the top. In effect, the participants *become* those objects. Then the group tries to tell the story of a use case with the participants/objects working as a team to supply the necessary information. These sessions are very fun, and they provide tremendous insight into ways the objects can collaborate effectively to achieve the desired results of the use cases. The traceability back to use cases is very clear in CRC card sessions. The stories told are the use case paths, and the results of the CRC card sessions are input into the analysis or design model.

8.1.4 Test Model Traceability

REFERENCE: RUP (test model artifact)

One of the clearest traceability links is between use cases and test models. After all, it is fairly obvious when you take a step back that use cases *are* test cases, just moved to the front of the lifecycle and called requirements.

The test plan will likely be organized by use case. The test scenarios will add test data to the use cases to become testable. The test cases will focus on each use case path.

8.1.5 User Interface Design Traceability

User interface design comes from the requirements, including use cases and usability. (For more information about nonfunctional requirement traceability see Section 8.2.) The user interface storyboards use use cases as their "stories," showing how the screen mock-ups progress as a fictional user walks through a use case.

8.1.6 Application Architecture Traceability

REFERENCE: RUP (software architecture document)

Application architecture provides the foundation for how the components and objects are organized in the target technical environment. As its input, use cases help to identify the *control objects or components*. Control objects are the objects that manage the other objects into transactions that are useful to users. Those transactions are patterned after use cases.

8.1.7 Project Management Traceability

REFERENCE: Chapter 7 in this book

Project management in an iterative/incremental project is focused on the production of use cases, meaning that the team works to create working, tested code that automates the stories told in the use cases. We have much more detail on project management in Chapter 7 of this book.

8.1.8 Documentation and Training Traceability

An often-overlooked traceability opportunity on software projects is into documentation and training. The ways the users will want to learn about using the application will be by use case (assuming the use cases are constructed correctly). They will want to learn one story at a time, stories told from their perspectives. Therefore, it makes sense to organize end user training courses and user documentation by use case. This approach also allows documentation and training professionals to fit in effectively into the iterative/incremental lifecycle. Their documentation and training artifacts can be pieced together one use case at a time as the development team attacks each use case.

8.1.9 Product Marketing Traceability

In software product companies, use cases become an effective marketing tool. As new releases of the software go into general availability, the marketing team has a useful list of the new stories they can tell with the product and subsequently new sections for product demonstration scripts.

8.1.10 Security Traceability

Use cases begin by examining the goals of the actors. The actor definitions provide the basis for creating security profiles. If the actor definitions are defined in the way the users use the application, the actor definitions trace smoothly into security user groups. Similarly, the use cases are the ways the actors use the application, so they effectively become the resources that are assigned to the user groups.

8.1.11 Release Planning

When management of a product is planning a set of releases, it is useful to have a coarse-grained set of features that will go into each release. The most logical pieces to use for this type of planning are use cases. This applies to a software product team or an internal project for an IT shop.

8.2 Tracing Back to Nonfunctionals

Although traceability tends to focus mostly on use cases, other types of software requirements must be traceable into the development lifecycle. Nonfunctionals have traceability
that is unique from use cases, but just as important in their own way.

If use cases are the major *application traceable requirements*, nonfunctionals are the
major *architecture traceable requirements*. Nonfunctionals provide the scope for the architectural needs of the software.

In order to delve into how nonfunctionals provide a basis for software architecture, it
is worthwhile now to describe some aspects of architecture. Software architecture is the
underlying structure of software application(s). This underlying structure includes how
the applications are divided into components (called the *component architecture*), and the
common set of services (security, navigation, transaction handling, and so on) that many
parts of the application need (called the *architectural framework*).

The architecture is created to ensure the quality of the way the application responds to
the demands made of it by its users. The architecture does not usually provide functions or
features itself; instead it makes those functions and features better: faster, more secure, with
higher availability, and so on.

Nonfunctionals provide direction for the architecture because they specify how fast,
how secure, and how available the application must be to fulfill the business needs. If a
nonfunctional requirement states that a software application must have 24×7 availability
99.999% of the time, this is a very strenuous requirement. An architect may need to construct a fairly heavy-duty architecture to comply with this architecture, including multiple
failover servers, complex load-balancing software to balance the load between the servers,
and several other methods of quick recovery from component failures. This will cost a lot
of money to design, purchase, construct, and test the hardware and software components.

Businesspeople seem to have an interesting relationship with nonfunctional requirements. With features, and therefore use cases, they seem to understand and appreciate that
each one costs money. Nonfunctionals, however, are often viewed by businesspeople as
"free of charge." They see a Microsoft Access application that has the features they need and
expect it to scale to a thousand-user base without a problem! However, we know that these
nonfunctional requirements cost money, often a lot of money. We like to tell our business
stakeholders that if they want infinite availability (true 24×7) *it will cost infinitely*. The
same is true for any other nonfunctional.

Similarly, the way a software architecture is tested is by creating load/stress test cases
based on the nonfunctionals. Perhaps a nonfunctional states that the software must handle
a load of 500 users while consistently providing a response time of less than 3 seconds per
interaction. The test team can create a set of test cases to simulate this condition, probably
using a load testing tool like Mercury Interactive LoadRunner to create virtual users to load
the servers as if 500 people were accessing it simultaneously.

Nonfunctional requirements also help provide input to software architects to understand the architectural patterns they may want to use. Some examples of architectural patterns include data-centered, repository, blackboard, pipes-and-filters, publish-and-subscribe, rules engine, and so on. These patterns are described in the book *Software Architecture in Practice* (Bass 1998).

We cannot provide a guide to translating nonfunctional requirements to architectural patterns. The book we've mentioned has some insights into this art (not science), but for the most part the task simply requires an experienced software architect or talented architecture mentors.

From a product marketing perspective, nonfunctionals play an important role. In a market where several products provide similar functions, nonfunctionals may be the key to winning market share. For instance, if several data translation tools offer the same functions (use cases), the winner may be the one who does it fastest, most securely, or can operate in a multithreaded mode.

8.3 Tracing Back to Business Rules

Business rules are also traceable into lifecycle artifacts. Business rules are, by their nature, constraints. As they move into software design, business rules become constraints on the class diagram. Here are the mappings for each type of business rule.

8.3.1 Structural Facts

Structural facts often become attributes of classes on the class diagram. They also become entries in a data dictionary or glossary as the project proceeds. Structural facts generally cannot be tested in test cases.

8.3.2 Action-Restricting and Action-Triggering Rules

Action-restricting rules usually become constraints on the class diagram. Constraints are restrictions on the associations between classes. Action-triggering rules are also indicated on the associations as association names and roles. Action-restricting and action-triggering rules are tested in test cases.

8.3.3 Calculations and Inferences

Calculations and inferences become details of the operations of the classes. They may be translated into detailed design activity diagrams or directly into program code. Calculations and inferences are tested using test cases.

9

Good judgment comes from
experience and experience
comes from bad judgment.

—FREDERICK P. BROOKS

Classic Mistakes

Some mistakes are classic.

9.1 Mistakes, Pitfalls, and Bruised Knees

Making mistakes is the biggest part of learning. To bolster the learning process, great managers encourage their teams to make mistakes early and often. Whether encouraged or not, we've always strived to get on with the mistakes so that we can reach the point at which we're doing things better.

In this chapter, we point out the mistakes we've made or that we've observed others making. Our main reason is not to help you avoid making these mistakes; you'll make them anyway. Instead, our aim is to help you recognize the mistakes when you make them and to help you move quickly to other ways of doing things. The preceding chapters have been "what to do." This chapter is "what to do and then move on."

9.2 Classic Mistakes: Make Them and Move On

Tables 9.1 through 9.7 describe the classic mistakes people make when they're gathering and specifying requirements, particularly those mistakes related to use cases. The tables are organized into general areas: perspective, thriftiness, messiness, overengineering, mismanagement, context, and notation. You can use them as a reference, and perhaps it would be good to bring them out from time to time to remind the team of the usual mistakes that happen. If you and your team tend to err in a particular way—say, overengineering—you can put more focus on that section in your discussions.

Table 9.1 Classic Mistakes of Perspective

Number	Classic Mistake	Issues and Concerns	Related Sections
001	Creating inside-out use cases	It is easy for developers to create inside-out use cases, which operate from the perspective of the application and not the user. The problem is that users often don't understand this perspective because it is not natural for them.	2.3.1.2 No Implementation-Specific Language
002	Including user interface details in use cases	Embedding user interface details in use cases is actually quite acceptable—after requirements have been gathered. But during requirements gathering, keep user interface details out. They serve only as a distraction from the interactions that need to occur.	1.5.4 Prototypes 2.3.1.2 No Implementation-Specific Language
003	Expanding the system boundary	It is difficult to keep in mind the scope of the system you're developing. For example, if a security identification system is connected to your application, is it inside the boundary? Or is it an actor? Or should it not be shown on use case diagrams? It depends on whether this project team is responsible for implementing and testing it. If it is an integrated component, it's inside the boundary and not shown in the use case diagram. If it is a separate system done by a separate team, it becomes an actor.	2.3.2.1 Actors and Roles
004	Creating use case interactions that don't provide value to an actor	Use cases must generally provide value to an actor. The actor doesn't necessarily have to be the same one who provides the input for the use case.	2.3.1.1 Interactions That Provide Value to Actors

Table 9.2 Classic Mistakes of Thriftiness

Number	Classic Mistake	Issues and Concerns	Related Sections
001	Skipping iterations	There is a tendency to skip iterations in requirements, especially for those coming from a big-bang waterfall mind-set. For very small projects, it may sometimes make sense, but usually it is wise to go through the four iterations or at least to address all the individual steps detailed in the iteration chapters if fewer iterations are required.	Chapter 4, The Facade Iteration Chapter 5, The Filled Iteration Chapter 6, The Focused Iteration
002	Skipping interview notes that don't fit	If some requirements from the interviews don't fit into the current iteration, people tend to skip them, thinking that they'll come back in the iteration they're supposed to. They might not! Keep free-form notes that don't fit the use cases or business rules of the current iteration and review these notes during each subsequent iteration.	Chapter 4, The Facade Iteration Chapter 5, The Filled Iteration Chapter 6, The Focused Iteration
003	Holding on to use cases that don't belong	Thrifty people hate to throw things away. However, extraneous use cases or business rules that don't belong should be tossed. Version control is helpful here. Throw things away. If you need them later, you can go back a version or two and retrieve them.	Chapter 7, Managing Requirements and People

Table 9.3 Classic Mistakes of Messiness

Number	Classic Mistake	Issues and Concerns	Related Sections
001	Keeping temporary requirements lists	A common mistake is to keep a contraband list of requirements off to the side and then incorporate the requirements into the use cases as they make sense. This means you're doing the work twice; the second time you're just changing the format of the requirements from a list to use cases. This is an acceptable first step into the world of use cases, but it should not become a practice, simply because it is extra work.	Chapter 1, The Trouble with Requirements Chapter 3, A Use-Case-Driven Approach to Requirements Gathering
002	Grouping use cases or business rules poorly	It helps a lot to group the use cases, but this is difficult to do. Group use cases and business rules in ways that make sense to the stakeholders. Group use cases using UML packages. Group business rules using category columns in the business rules catalog.	Chapter 7, Managing Requirements and People
003	Having use cases without an owner	Each use case should have an owner. Use cases that are not assigned ownership are often not modified consistently throughout the iterations.	Chapter 7, Managing Requirements and People
004	Having use cases with too many owners	A use case that has too many owners will die a death no less painful than those use cases without any owner. No one really owns it, and people make contradictory changes to the use case, wasting precious time.	Chapter 7, Managing Requirements and People

continues

Table 9.3 continued

Number	Classic Mistake	Issues and Concerns	Related Sections
005	Including too many cross-references in use case text	Some use case textbooks list various ancillary sections in their use case templates that duplicate information from the use case diagram or other places. Don't include these sections. This is duplicate work that you will have to spend time modifying when things change later in the life-cycle or during maintenance. Here is a subset of these sections: actor lists, included use cases, activity diagrams, user interface, sequence diagrams, subordinate use cases, participating classes. Two exceptions: a primary actor (just one) and extension points.	2.3.3 The Use Case Template
006	Not keeping use cases and business rules in a database	The need to cross-reference, sort, and list the use case titles and business rules means that a database or spread-sheet is the most appropriate place for use cases, especially for a large system.	Chapter 7, Managing Requirements and People
007	Trying to build extensive exception logic into the basic course of events	The purpose of the Exception Paths section in the template is to document paths that occur when something goes wrong. Don't try to put all this in the Basic Course of Events section.	2.3.1.2 No Implementation-Specific Language 2.3.1.3 User-Appropriate Level of Detail 2.3.3 The Use Case Template

Table 9.4 Classic Mistakes of Overengineering

Number	Classic Mistake	Issues and Concerns	Related Sections
001	Neglecting useful tools within use cases	A use case does not have to be text only. Within a use case, it is perfectly acceptable, even encouraged, to have diagrams, tables, flowcharts, or any other graphic representation that best tells what is happening in the use case. Decision tables for complex logic are a great example.	2.3.3 The Use Case Template
002	Creating CRUD use cases first	CRUD table maintenance is often an acceptable use case, but these use cases should not be the first ones you work on. The first use cases to be created should be those that provide the most value to the actors. CRUD value is almost always subordinate to the major business processes.	
003	Using computer terminology in use cases	During the requirements activity, all use cases should be in language that the users understand. No computer terminology (LANs, WANs, GUI elements, servers, workstations, screens, windows, and so on) should be used.	2.3.1.2 No Implementation-Specific Language
004	Writing pseudocode for use case text	Use cases are descriptions of interactions between actors and an application. They are not pseudocode or code. They should be written in English (or Spanish or French) and not in OCL, OQL, or anything else remotely machine-readable	2.3.1.2 No Implementation-Specific Language 2.3.3 The Use Case Template

continues

165

Table 9.4 continued

Number	Classic Mistake	Issues and Concerns	Related Sections
005	Assuming that the *extend* relationships between use cases dictate class inheritance in design	This is more a mistake of analysis or design. It is natural to assume that the *extend* relationships shown in the use cases will translate into inheritance relationships in a class diagram. There is no correlation between *extend* and class inheritance in design.	
006	Assuming that the *include* relationships between use cases dictate class responsibilities in design	This is a mistake of analysis or design (or both). It is natural to assume that the *include* relationships shown in the use cases will translate to specific classes that should be extracted and assigned specific responsibilities. There is no correlation between *include* and class creation or responsibility assignment in design.	
007	Confusing actors with specific people or organizational positions	Actors are roles. One person might play several roles, and one role might be played by several people. To avoid redesigns when organizational or staffing changes occur, you should not couple actor definitions to specific people or organizational positions.	2.3.2.1 Actors and Roles
008	Making business process assumptions that are not verified	There's the way things should work, and then there's the way they do work. While you're creating use cases and business rules, verify, verify, verify. Common sense has nothing to do with it.	Chapter 4, The Facade Iteration Chapter 5, The Filled Iteration Chapter 6, The Focused Iteration

Number	Classic Mistake	Issues and Concerns	Related Sections
009	Putting everything into one use case diagram	This is extremely common. Why not show every possible use case in one diagram and depict the relationships between all? This is a classic mistake because it is too much for users to take in all at once. Instead, break the system into use case packages, show all packages on one diagram, and then break down the packages into use cases.	5.2.1.2 Review Use Case Granularity
010	Putting everything into one use case	There should be one use case that describes the entire application: the system context use case. However, it should be at such an abstract level that it is useful only as a general scope statement. Some system context use cases contain a Basic Course of Events that is pages and pages long. This is an abstraction mismatch and should not be done. No use cases should have more than two pages of text for the basic course of events.	5.2.1.2 Review Use Case Granularity
011	Abstracting too much	What? We've been telling you to abstract all along! Can you have too much of a good thing? Of course. How do you tell? Ask your users. If you've abstracted the functionality to such a degree that your users don't understand it anymore, it's too much.	5.3.4 Abstraction Filter
012	Using IF-THEN-ELSEs in the use cases	Pseudocode in use cases can make users uncomfortable.	5.2.2.7 Document Exceptions
013	Creating hierarchies of use cases	This is a holdover from the "bad ole days" of functional decomposition. All use cases should be created at the same level of detail. Don't create "high level" use cases and then "more detailed" and "really detailed." You'll lose perspective on the original business problem.	4.3.2 The Hierarchy Killer

Table 9.5   Classic Mistakes of Mismanagement

Number	Classic Mistake	Issues and Concerns	Related Sections
001	Trying to force simultaneous iterations	Iterations can certainly overlap. However, we've known several managers who think that everything should happen at the same time because it makes their project plans end by the date promised to management. This is the wrong reason. Let iterations overlap naturally, but don't force the issue or a lot will fall through the cracks. If iterations are happening simultaneously, there should be separate teams per iteration.	
002	Allowing an imbalance between experience and inexperience	In requirements gathering, a few inexperienced analysts often get paired with too few experienced analysts. Worse yet, no one has business knowledge. Requirements are the most pivotal artifact of the lifecycle. Reduce your investment in them at your peril.	Chapter 7, Managing Requirements and People
003	Packaging use cases too late	Use case packages are your tool for reducing complexity on diagrams. Use them early and often. If there is a set of functionality that you don't need to deal with right now, lump it into a package and let it sit until the time is right.	5.2.1.2 Review Use Case Granularity
004	Using packages to hide complexity that you're trying to avoid	The purpose of packages is to hide complexity. However, if you use packages of use cases to hide a part of the system that you don't yet understand, you're only putting off the inevitable task of learning that part of the application. If you put it off until later in the requirements activity, you risk running past your deadline when the package turns out to be a lot more complex than you originally thought.	4.3.7 Packages as Placeholders for Functionality

Table 9.6 Classic Mistakes of Context

Number	Classic Mistake	Issues and Concerns	Related Sections
001	Confusing *include*, *precondition*, and *assumption*	As long as you use consistent definitions of these three terms, your use cases will be meaningful. We've provided some definitions that make sense to us, but you can use your own, as long as they're applied consistently. And, to be safe, steer clear of include and extend unless you are extending an earlier release of a product and don't want to change the original use cases.	5.3.2 IPA Filter
002	Using two columns in the Basic Course of Events section in use case template	This is quite common, and it is even advocated in some textbooks. Here's the question to answer. Usually use cases are interactions between one actor and the application. What happens when multiple actors get involved? Do you then create three columns? Or put both actors in the left column? This seems like a good idea until you try it in complex situations.	2.3.3 The Use Case Template
003	Confusing *include* and *extend*	Confusing the use case adornments is very common. Remember, *includes* (formerly *uses*) is like a function call; *extends* is like inheritance.	2.3.2.2 Associations
004	Underusing use cases during the lifecycle	We believe that use cases are extremely useful after requirements gathering is complete.	Chapter 8 Requirements Traceability

Table 9.7 Classic Mistakes of Notation

Number	Classic Mistake	Issues and Concerns	Related Sections
001	Using use cases as scenarios	It's easy to confuse use cases with scenarios. Use cases represent a fairly abstract actor interaction that provides value to the actor. Scenarios are instantiated from use cases and provide specific interactions with specific value.	2.3.4 Paths and Scenarios
002	Using weak verbs in use case names	Use case names are extremely important because they identify the interaction. Poor names are usually too vague or misleading.	4.3.5 Verb Filter
003	Using weak nouns in use cases	Nouns that are computer-specific or just plain bland not only do not help with interpretation of the use case text but also point to vague areas of understanding by the requirements analyst.	4.3.6 Noun Filters
004	Portraying application parts as actors	It is common for analysts familiar with only part of the application to take another section of the application and put it outside the boundary of the use case as an actor. This is right only when the outside application part is not the responsibility of this team.	2.3.2.1 Actors and Roles
005	Underusing pre-conditions and postconditions	Preconditions and postconditions provide an excellent scope management feature for use case creation. If the analyst, the user, and the project manager agree on the preconditions and postconditions for a use case, the analyst is free to find the steps that take the use case from the before to the after. Preconditions and postconditions provide the analyst with a liberating structure.	2.3.3 The Use Case Template

Number	Classic Mistake	Issues and Concerns	Related Sections
006	Using secondary actors inappropriately	Secondary actors should be shown on use case diagrams when the application is likely to require information about them—that is, when the secondary actors are likely to become classes in the class diagram during analysis and design.	2.3.2.1 Actors and Roles
007	Forgetting that actors can become classes	During analysis and design, the classes that provide the values in use cases are designed and assigned responsibilities. However, actors also become classes when it is important to store information about those actors.	2.3.2.1 Actors and Roles
008	Overusing adornments	The inherent mistake here is thinking of a use case diagram as a system design or data design. It's not. If the adornments (*extend, include,* and so on) are starting to clutter the use case diagram, it probably means that the mind-set of the team needs to be pointed toward requirements instead of design.	2.3.2.2 Associations
009	Confusing who extends whom	It is easy to confuse the extender with the extendee. The specialization use case should be at the blunt end of the arrow, and the general use case should be at the sharp end of the arrow.	2.3.2.2 Associations

10

The Case for Use Cases

Use cases, as descriptions, have become very popular, ever since the first edition of our book. They have been applied in many ways that the original use case team may not have envisaged. They have certainly become the *gold standard* for capturing requirements for software applications.

Some people think use cases can be used for anything.
Is it a hammer looking for a nail?

173

In this chapter, we summarize why we believe use cases are now so widely used as requirements artifacts for software. We also briefly explore some of the other ways use cases have been applied and how successful these uses have been. In particular, we focus on two areas: business use cases and service use cases.

10.1 Why Did Use Cases Win?

When we wrote the first edition of *Use Cases: Requirements in Context*, it was far from obvious that use cases would become popular in capturing software requirements. As our book gained in popularity, and other use case books were subsequently written and became successful, we realized that this was a real revolution in software process. Many, many corporations have standardized on use-case-driven lifecycles. Today, it is difficult to find Fortune 1000 IT departments where use cases are not used in some form or fashion. Although we are not surprised at the fact that people find use cases useful, we have been taken aback by the surge in popularity in an industry where flash usually wins over substance.

But why did use cases win the requirements war? We feel there are several reasons:

- Use cases are sensible to businesspeople.
- Use cases are traceable.
- Use cases are an excellent scoping tool.
- Use cases don't use a special language.
- Use cases allow us to tell stories.
- The alternatives are awful.

10.1.1 Use Cases Are Sensible to Businesspeople

An amazing feature of use cases is that businesspeople tend to understand them fairly quickly, regardless of the businessperson's technical abilities. There are several reasons that this occurs. First, businesspeople prefer to read specifications written as sentences and paragraphs, not as diagrams or pseudocode. Although most people are visually oriented, diagrams created by technical people tend to overwhelm businesspeople. These diagrams include every possibility of a process, all the "else" sides of every possibility and all the "hardly ever happens" stuff mixed in with the basic stuff.

Use cases, by their design, tend to simplify the picture by isolating the "basic path" from all the peripheral, confusing twists and bends of a "complete" business process.

Each use case represents one business transaction. The way they are divided into separate pieces is along the lines of business thought, not technical subsystems. This makes it much easier for businesspeople to visualize each use case and its business goal.

10.1.2 Use Cases Are Traceable

We don't wish to rehash everything from Chapter 8, but we'd like to include traceability as an important benefit of use cases. Use cases are natural for businesspeople and are also natural for elaboration into technical artifacts. The stories in use cases naturally lead into the analysis, design, and testing artifacts providing an answer to the question: Are we working on what we are supposed to be working on?

Traceability, or lack of it, has been a major factor in software applications that are built, perhaps even within budget and ahead of schedule, but not matching business expectations. Use cases help solve that problem.

10.1.3 Use Cases Are an Excellent Scoping Tool

Use cases put the major focus of requirements on the boundary between what is in scope and what is out of scope. Use cases are the stories of what crosses the line between in and out. By creating this focus, they can create a clear division for scoping the project. Does this mean that every use-case-driven project has a tightly controlled scope? Unfortunately, no. But use cases are a requirements tool that help scope creep rather than hinder it.

10.1.4 Use Cases Don't Use a Special Language

Technical people who dabble with use cases usually tend to want to change them to make them, well, more technical. They want to use a language that is absolutely consistent, unambiguous, and even computer-readable. Imagine feeding the requirements of an application into a tool and *out comes the code*! However, there's one hitch. Once the use cases become computer readable, they are no longer businessperson-readable. Even when certain words are capitalized (*IF the limit is reached AND the status is PREFERRED*) the use cases begin to look more like computer code than stories. Businesspeople understand stories, but not computer code. The strength of use cases is also the weakness—English language (or Chinese, German, and so on). The vagaries and problems of our written language come with the territory if we want documents that are readable by a wide audience. Since business analysts who create use cases recognize that, they have a better chance at producing requirements that won't just sit on a shelf.

10.1.5 Use Cases Allow Us to Tell Stories

Much of the fun in life is about stories. Telling jokes, reading fiction, dating, journalism, sales, being friends, and most of the arts revolve around stories. Stories are a central part of life and culture around the world. Use cases give us an opportunity to tell stories about a new software application that does not yet exist. Is there a better way to share ideas about a future state than to tell each other stories? Stories wrap up a feeling of "being there" that no sterile list can supply.

Businesspeople can feel this. In fact, usually when we solicit requirements from businesspeople, no matter what tool we decide to use, they relay information to IT people using stories. It is very natural when we respond to them with software requirements that those requirements would also be expressed through stories.

Generally, technical people harbor some disdain for the idea of "stories" in a software lifecycle. However, businesspeople take stories very seriously. I remember a businessperson telling me the virtues of *Fortune* magazine over *Forbes* (or vice versa, I don't remember) because it had "more stories about people's successes." Businesspeople may seem to be interested in cold facts and figures, but the way they really learn is through stories.

A recent business book called *The Dream Society* (Jensen 2001) has this focus. It states that the businesses that will break through the cacophony of advertising and marketing to succeed will be those that have compelling stories. People can relate to the poor young boy who worked his way up from a busboy to create a great food service corporation. Or the woman who was laid off from a major corporation only to begin a thriving holistic health business. In the future, the book states, those companies with a story to tell will profit and all others will struggle. After the Information Society, he says, comes the Dream Society. The society of stories.

10.1.6 The Alternatives Are Awful

As we discussed in Chapter 1, there aren't any good alternatives to use cases, at least none that we've seen. Contract-style requirements lists are troublesome. They are readable by businesspeople but have no traceability into analysis, design, and testing artifacts. Dataflow diagrams, functional decompositions, and entity-relationship diagrams do not sit well with business stakeholders and users. They cannot relate an abstract diagram to a software application to be built. So use cases, for all their shortcomings, are currently our best alternatives.

10.2 Use Cases Beyond Software

Use cases have fulfilled the role of software requirements well. Perhaps because of that fact, use cases have moved into other areas that have had problems in notation. Two applications of use cases we'll examine here are *service use cases* and *business use cases.*

10.2.1 Service Use Cases

A great example of use cases being applied to a pressing business problem is the emergence of *service use cases.* Lance Tracy, a pioneer in this field based in California, has done work for several companies to help them define the services they offer to their clients with use cases as his central tool.

As a company is defining (or redefining itself), a series of questions must be addressed:

1. What is the vision of this company?
2. What is its mission?
3. How do we define the business we are in?
4. What are the services we provide to our customers?

In response to the last question, the team creates use cases for each service they intend to offer to their customers. The customer is the actor, and substantial effort goes into defining that actor (the *target market* in marketing terms). Then they examine two critical components of Service Use Cases: the goals of each actor (what a customer wishes to accomplish when he or she deals with the company) and the service level agreement (SLA) that must be met (basic agreements the company can provide to a customer regarding the performance of services). An SLA is essentially a set of nonfunctional requirements for a set of service offerings. If an internal IT group agrees to offer a set of services to the company's business groups, it is likely to set up an SLA to govern what it means to offer "acceptable service." This includes defining how fast the services will be completed, the level of customer service, and so on. These agreements are very similar to how nonfunctionals describe how fast a computer system will offer its services to its users.

Once this framework of goals and standards is established, they begin to define service use cases, the interactions between the customer actor and the company's "system" (system of processes, not necessarily software) that provides customers with what they want, how they want it, and when they want it. The team then elaborates these service use cases into internal business processes that will satisfy those criteria set out in the service use cases.

The use of service use cases also helps training efforts for service offerings in a company. For instance, instructional designers do something called "front end analysis," where they ask similar questions to what a person creating service use cases would ask:

- What is the participant's goal?
- What sequence of steps do we take to accomplish that goal?
- How will we know when we are done?
- How will the participant know that he or she has completed the task correctly?

Lance and his teams have also used the service use case process to uncover hidden costs in existing service offerings and to identify labor issues that could cause problems later in the company's life.

We like how use cases provide a tremendous amount of focus for the often fuzzy process of service definition. Since such a big percentage of Western economies are made up of service companies, and even product companies are turning themselves into service companies, the timeliness of Lance's approach is good. Service use cases are in their infancy at the moment, but we're certain they'll catch on and replace many of the older methodologies of reorganizing companies and their service offerings once people see how use cases bring such focus to the task.

10.2.2 Business Use Cases

Related to service use cases but different are *business use cases*. Business use cases describe business processes, similar to how process diagrams or flowcharts have been used. But there is an important difference. Business use cases define business processes from the outside in, beginning with the external *business actors*: customers, suppliers, partners, non-profit partners, shareholders, and so on. The business process team examines the goals of these "business actors" and then identifies the ways these actors want to interact with the business in order to achieve those goals. Those interactions become use cases, but the "business" is treated like a black box, where we don't care *how* the business provides the right reactions to the actors, only that it does (the same way we treated the software in software use cases). Once those use cases are written, the team can begin to map the internal processes to satisfy those external actors' goals.

First, we should explain that when we say "the business," this could mean the entire organization (corporation, government department, and so on) or it could mean just one division of an organization (personnel, purchasing, shop floor, and so on). The place where the boundary is drawn is dictated by the scope of the project. If the project team has been tasked with reorganizing the entire company, then "the business," and therefore the black box, is drawn around the entire company. But if it is meant to reorganize only one department, say Purchasing, then the box is around Purchasing. This means that anyone outside Purchasing who needs to interact with Purchasing to fulfill a goal (vendors, other departments, company executives, and so on) is a business actor. The team will examine the goals of each actor and then identify business use cases that fulfill those goals, and finally create internal processes (perhaps using UML sequence diagrams) to show what has to happen internally to satisfy the business actors' goals.

There is an important benefit that use cases provide in this process over other methods. Since use cases are focused on the goals of the external parties, they can help provide some abstraction away from the "as is" view of the internal business processes. By treating the department (or company) as a black box initially, it is easier to try to imagine "in a perfect world" what the absolute best results are that we could provide to the actors. Then our job is to create internal processes that satisfy those goals. This is a completely different perspective than simply examining internal processes step-by-step and trying to find incremental improvements by looking for places where we can take out steps or do things faster. It gives the organization a much more "stakeholder-driven" style, whether the stakeholders are the customers, partners, or company executives. The difference can be dramatic.

10.2.2.1 Challenges of Business Processes

As software gets more involved in business processes, the auditing function for a business is likely to ask for a completely auditable process no matter whether the process is carried out by a human being or a piece of software. Since a business auditor is not necessarily computer literate, the proper auditability of the process with the involved software is a key business concern.

If we also consider the fact that the business process in question may have to change, a reasonable requirement for the software involved will be its flexibility, or configurability. That is, it should be able to be reconfigured according to the changing structure or at least the changing parameters of the process. Note that this is business process configuration and it is not just another nonfunctional requirement for the software. In order to identify and develop the needed solutions in a changing business environment, another form of requirements documentation must be introduced to capture the necessary business requirements with the bigger picture, that is, complete and end-to-end business processes, which present the solutions to business needs.

Once the needed information of the business processes is included into the use-case-based requirements, this inclusion will provide necessary specifications on both why and how the software should be installed and maintained in the context of the business solution. The understanding of the usage of the software in the "real world" context will enable the IT professionals involved (business analysts, architects, developers, testers, and so on) to develop better software.

The IT professionals who are directly involved in software development are not the only beneficiaries of the business use cases. A business use case that relates the IT functions to process context is also an educational tool that demonstrates not only the business value of the IT package, but also how the package should be operated to support the values for the end users.

10.2.2.2 Features of Business Use Cases

Table 10.1 shows a sample business use case. Business use cases share these common attributes with system use cases:

- A business use case focuses on end-to-end business processes. It must provide concrete business reasons to get started and business consequences or values to end.
- A business use case focuses on interactions between all parties involved, no matter if it is a human being or a software system. Therefore, it requires identification of all business actors including the need for IT support.
- A business use case focuses on identifying the responsibilities of all business actors in the context of the business process from end to end. The functions of the IT system to be developed are a subset of the scope identified in the business use cases.
- A business use case focuses on identifying the business information contents in the context of the business process from end to end. The information processed by the software systems to be developed is a subset of the contents identified in the business use cases.

Once we have captured the business information in the form of business use cases, we can easily start developing our system use cases as a result. Note that the requirement development process between business use cases and system use cases is not a waterfall approach. Iterations between business use cases and system use cases will be needed to

Table 10.1   Review Leasing Document Business Use Case

Basic Flow	The use case begins when the Portfolio Manager wants to review the lease document after being notified by the Investment Manager that the document has been completed.
1. Retrieve the Leasing Application.	The system retrieves and displays the leasing document.
2. Review the Leasing Application.	The Portfolio Manager reviews the system specification and legal terms of the leasing application.
3. Retrieve the Credit History of the Applicant.	The system retrieves and displays the credit history of the applicant.
4. Review the Credit History of the Applicant.	The Portfolio Manager reviews the credit history.
5. Application Acceptable.	The Portfolio Manager accepts the application and notifies the Investment Manager. The use case terminates.
Alternate Flows	
The Legal Terms Unacceptable	If in step 2 of the Basic Flow the Portfolio Manager finds the legal terms unacceptable, the Portfolio Manager will notify the Investment Manager of the reasons for rejection. The use case terminates.
The Credit History Disqualified	If in step 4 of the Basic Flow, the Portfolio Manager finds that the credit history of the applicant disqualifies the applicant, the Portfolio Manager will notify the Investment Manager of the reasons for rejection. The use case terminates.
The System Specification Unacceptable	If in steps 2 or 4 of the Basic Flow the Portfolio Manager finds the system specification unacceptable, the Portfolio Manager will notify the Investment Manager of the reasons for rejection. The use case terminates.

facilitate the process of specifying the best possible business solution as well as the software systems that support the solution.

10.3 Summary

This book has advocated use cases for software requirements and other things as well. We feel that use cases are an important tool in helping people take a hard look at what they want from something, whether it's a piece of software, a department, service offering, or even a new kitchen. The "black box" approach of use cases makes them especially useful. It's likely that other techniques will come along that are even better in this or other ways, but for now we have use cases. Thanks for reading our book. Feel free to e-mail us anytime:

Daryl Kulak   daryl@simplicity-institute.com

Eamonn Guiney   ucbook@eguiney.com

A

Real Estate Management System

A.1 Overview

We use the example of a real estate management system to illustrate the development of a full-sized system-requirements analysis. As with the other examples, we reduce the complexity to fit within the context of this book by ignoring some details and whole requirements, making the requirements presented here an illustration of the use case methodology without being, necessarily, a complete real estate management system. There are whole sets of requirements that are out of the scope of this book, including the accounting functionality that must underpin a system such as this.

As we present this analysis, we emphasize the changes that take place in our understanding of the system, as reflected by the use cases, and try to reduce the duplication usually visible when the results of an incremental process is displayed linearly in an appendix.

The basis of this system is this: an investor allocates a percentage of assets to real estate. In this case, he purchases or builds commercial real estate such as shopping malls and office buildings. These assets require management just like a portfolio of fixed income securities. To reduce the use of spreadsheets as the management tool, the investor requires a system to automate the recording and reporting on these investments. Specifically, the scope of this system should include the ability to track the capital allocations made and provisioned, the resulting cash flows for the property and the sources for these cash flows, and the ability to calculate the return on these investments.

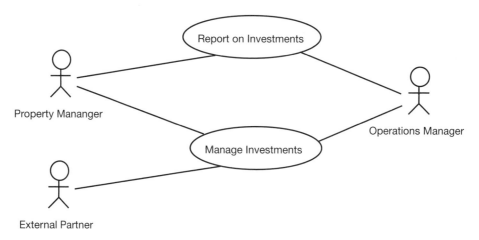

Figure A.1   *Initial Scope*

Our first step is to think about the broad scope of this system.

We identified two use cases initially: "manage investments" and "report on investments." We also identified three actors: the operations manager, the property manager, and the external partner.

We worked with the key stakeholders to document the following high-level technical and functional requirements.

A.2 The Use Cases

Use Case Name:	Manage Investments
Description:	Track the essential attributes of properties the company invests in, the properties' tenants, and the leases
Actors:	• Property manager • Operations manager • External partner
Triggers:	Changes are made to the property portfolios, their tenants, or the leases.
Preconditions:	Categorization and other data is available to the system.

Use Case A.1   *Manage Investments (continues)*

Basic Course of Events:	1. When a property is acquired
	   a. Enter essential details of an investment (property)
	   b. Establish the capital commitments for the property
	   c. Divide the property into one or more units
	2. When a tenant is found for a property unit
	   a. Enter tenant details
	   b. Establish lease parameters
	   c. Establish the anticipated cash flow schedule
	   d. Associate the property unit with the tenant
	3. When a property is disposed of
	   a. Record the details of the sale
	   b. Disassociate all tenants from the property
	   c. Remove all future capital committed to the property
	   d. Remove all future cash flows from the schedule
	4. When a lease terminates
	   a. Disassociate the unit(s) from the tenant to make them available for future leases
	   b. Remove any future cash flows associated with the tenant

Exceptions:	None
Postconditions:	None

Use Case A.1   *continued*

Use Case Name:	Report on Investments
Description:	Collate stored data into a set of reports used to support business operations and decision making.
Actors:	• Property manager • Operations manager
Triggers:	• Property managers run reports mainly on an ad hoc basis to make a variety of decisions. • Operations managers run reports regularly to support business operations.

Use Case A.2   *Report on Investments (continues)*

Preconditions:	• Investments/Properties have had their details entered into the system. • Data from external sources must be acquired for the system for reports that rely on external data to be available.

Basic Course of Events:	1. The system displays a list of available reports, including
	    a. Operations reports
	       i. Leases expiring in n months
	       ii. Property utilization
	       iii. Open units per MSA
	    b. Property manager reports
	       i. Expected rate of return
	       ii. Top ten properties
	       iii. Properties per MSA
	       iv. Exposure
	    Note that this is not an exhaustive set of reports, but of the reports that are of most importance initially.
	2. The actor selects a report.
	3. The system prompts the actor for details to refine the report, including reporting date.
	4. The system retrieves data, performs calculations to derive data that is not stored, and applies sorting order.
	5. The system prepares the report for presentation including how the report looks and the delivery format (onscreen or print).

Exceptions:	None
Postconditions:	The system alters no business data based on report production.

Use Case A.2 *continued*

A.2.1 The Actors

A.2.1.1 Operations Manager

The operations manager is responsible for the data entry and data maintenance. The operations manager creates reports to provide management information regarding a property and ensures that the day-to-day issues with the properties are taken care of.

A.2.1.2 Property Manager

The property manager is responsible for the performance of a sum of money made available to her for real estate investments. The property manager identifies real estate projects of various types, in which to invest. This actor is primarily interested in the capital needed for an investment and the comparison between the capital committed and the return generated.

A.2.1.3 External Partner

The external partner performs a similar role to the property manager but is external to the organization. He is involved with the properties, but has discretion in many areas. His primary responsibility is to ensure that the investments produce a return; he also is required to provide regular information to the property managers, including cash flow, reconciliation, and returns information.

A.2.2 Technical Requirements and Business Rules

At this point, we have no pressing technical requirements except to note that there may be remote access requirements for the external property manager actor. We have no business rules to document at this point.

A.3 Scope Decisions

Our definition of system context gives us sufficient basis to make a number of scope decisions with the stakeholders. The first is that the stakeholders direct us to design the system from the viewpoint of a user. This is an essential direction, as we had considered the complex business requirements that emanate from the accounting system that could underpin the system. The stakeholders require a strong accounting underpinning for their business, but are content to keep the two systems separate. There is little data duplicated between their book of record (accounting system) and the real estate system, and they decline the added expense of adding either accounting functionality or data integration between the two systems.

The second directive from the stakeholders is that they view the system to as a "collect and report system." The philosophy will be to build a system to collect data that implements the business rules they define with the dual objectives of making this data "safe" (it will not be lost or forgotten) and providing specialized views of the data for various actors to make business decisions against (for example, the ability to compare the returns across investments and the ability to know what buildings are historically underutilized from a leasing perspective).

Our next steps are to find out as much information about how the various actors want to interact with the system, and the capabilities they require from it. The results of this work lead us to expand our use cases to the following. We break up our use case diagram into three, for a better fit.

This expands the set of use cases from 2 to 23. When we approached the problem of eliciting these requirements, our initial take was that there would be requirements to collect regarding the data entry for both property and tenants, so we dug in that direction first to see what we would come up with.

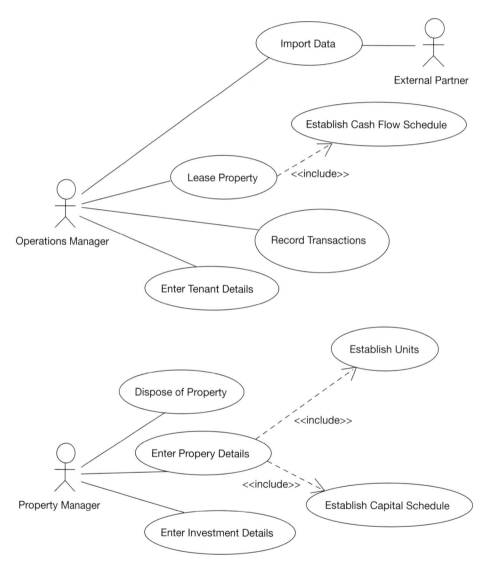

Figure A.2   *Data Entry Expanded*

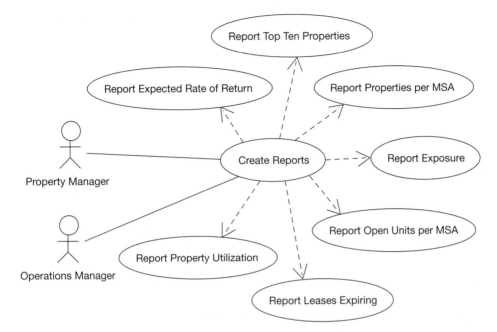

Figure A.3 *Reporting Expanded*

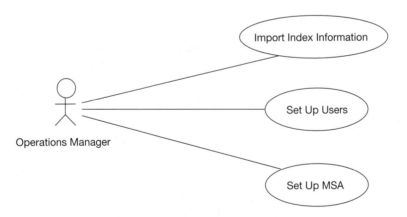

Figure A.4 *Maintenance Expanded*

A.3.1 List of Use Cases

Category	Use Case
Data Entry	Import Data
	Establish Cash Flow Schedule
	Lease Property
	Record Transactions
	Enter Tenant Details
	Dispose of Property
	Establish Units
	Enter Property Details
	Establish Capital Schedule
	Enter Investment Details
Reporting	Report Top Ten Properties
	Calculate Returns
	Report Properties per MSA
	Report Expected Rate of Return
	Report Exposure
	Create Reports
	Report Property Utilization
	Report Open Units per MSA
	Report Leases Expiring
Maintenance	Import Index Information
	Set Up MSA
	Set Up Users

Use Case Name:	**Enter Tenant Details**
Description:	The real estate system tracks who is leasing a property; the system stores a set of details of each tenant (lease holder) for billing, tracking, and exposure reasons.
Actors:	Operations manager
Triggers:	• A new tenant or potential tenant has been found for a property lease. This could be initiated from the lease property use case. • Additional or changed information has been found for an existing tenant.
Preconditions:	None

Basic Course of Events:	1. The operations manager navigates to the tenant area.
	2. The operations manager enters the identification information for a tenant:
	   a. First name, last name, and SSN for an individual, or
	   b. Company name and federal tax ID for an institution or organization
	3. The system checks for existing matching entries.
	4. The system displays a data entry template that is populated with any existing information. The template differs for individuals and organizations.
	   <Insert list of data items required.>
	5. The operations manager enters each data item.
	6. The system validates data according to the data entry rules (dates, and so on).
	7. When satisfied with the data entry, the operations manager commits the changes.
	8. The system validates that the data set is complete.
	9. The system stores the changes and if validation passed, the tenant is marked as validated.

Exceptions:	3. If the system finds a duplicate, alert the actor and display the existing tenant record. 7. If the actor is not satisfied with the changes, he optionally may abandon the changes. The system reverts to the previously stored record, if one existed.

Use Case A.3 *Enter Tenant Details (continues)*

	8. If mandatory data is missing, the system alerts the actor and explains the omission. If the tenant refers to a current lessee (that is, a tenant with an active lease) and the system will not accept changes, that will cause the tenant to lose validation status.
Postconditions:	If the data is complete and valid, the system has a validated tenant.
Business Rules:	<Insert field and form level validation details.>
Technical Requirements:	• This functionality will be used from the main office only, as the operations manager does not work from other locations. • The set of the data needed about a tenant has changed several times during our business; the property manager will require the flexibility to add and remove direct and derived data regarding tenants. • It is anticipated that only one person will update a tenant at one time; the system does not need to support simultaneous updates to tenant information. • The system should store the history of all changes to tenants together with the identity of the actor making the changes and the date and time of the work.

Use Case A.3 *continued*

Use Case Name:	**Enter Investment Details**
Description:	This system tracks details of real estate investments with an emphasis on lease management. Each investment is made up of the capital committed to the project by the manager and the cash flow generated by leasing parts of the investment to individuals or organizations. Each investment could span several properties.
Actors:	• Property manager • Operations manager

Use Case A.4 *Enter Investment Details (continues)*

Triggers:	• A new investment is entered into. • Additional details of an investment become available. • Changes to investment details are required. • A property manager wants to review the details of an investment.
Preconditions:	None

Basic Course of Events:	1. The actor navigates to the investment details area.
	2. Investments are identified by a name and system-assigned number; the name sometimes relates to the name of a property.
	3. The actor selects the investment from a system-displayed list or enters a new investment name.
	4. If the system located the investment, it retrieves the details and displays them.
	5. The actor enters the following identifying details of the investment:
	   a. Name
	   b. Location
	   c. Category (Residential SFH, residential multi-family home, retail, or office)
	   d. Property manager (select from a displayed list)
	6. The actor enters the capital commitment schedule.
	7. The actor enters date, capital, source, amount, estimate high, estimate low, and notes.
	8. The actor enters free-form notes.
	9. The actor enters other details including any contract numbers and contacts for other people and companies involved in the investment.
	10. When the actor is satisfied with the changes, the actor commits them, and the system responds by checking that all mandatory information about a deal is entered.

Exceptions:	
Postconditions:	
Business Rules:	
Technical Requirements:	

Use Case A.4   *continued*

Use Case Name:	**Enter Property Details**
Description:	A property, related to an investment that is, or will be, managed by the company, needs to have details tracked. The use case is responsible for collecting this information. Properties are made unique by their address and the investment identity that created the property.
Actors:	Operations manager
Triggers:	• Use case Enter Investment Details. • Additional or changed information becomes available about a property.
Preconditions:	An investment has been made and entered that relates to a property.

Basic Course of Events:	1. The operations manager navigates to the property details area.
	2. The operations manager selects a property to work on, or chooses to create a new property. To locate an existing property the operations manager may
	   a. Select from a list of property names and addresses and associated investment identities
	   b. Search using property name, category, and address
	3. If the property is new, the system prompts the operations manager to enter a name and address and to select an investment.
	4. The system displays any data collected.
	5. The operations manager enters the following data:
	   a. Note: team needs to analyze and define the set of data being collected.
	   b. MSA (Metropolitan Statistical Area)
	6. If the operations manager wishes, the property may be divided into a set of one or more units.

Exceptions:	• The combination of property name, address, and investment must be unique. • The system checks the property address. If the address is used for an existing property, the system alerts the operations manager and asks if the properties are related by an investment.

Use Case A.5 *Enter Property Details (continues)*

Postconditions:	The property becomes available for reporting and leasing.
Business Rules:	An investment may include many properties. Each investment includes at least one unit.
Technical Requirements:	The list of MSAs must be kept up-to-date with data provided by the United States Postal Service. Currently all investments have been made within the United States.

Use Case A.5   *continued*

Use Case Name:	**Establish Units**
Description:	For the purposes of leasing, a property consists of one or more units. The definition of *units* is flexible within the system as the category of the investment causes it to change. For example, in a SFH (Single Family Home) development, a unit is a home/lot; in a shopping mall a unit is a store or a vendor kiosk location.
Actors:	Operations manager
Triggers:	• An existing property is having its units reevaluated and changed. • A new property is being leased.
Preconditions:	The property exists in a system.

Basic Course of Events:	1. The operations manager navigates to the units area from the Enter Property Details use case.
	2. The operations manager reviews the set of units already established (by default there will be at least one).
	3. The operations manager chooses to add, modify, or delete a unit.
	4. The system prompts the operations manager for the following information:
	  a. Unit identity
	  b. Unit description (for example, lot number)
	  c. Size in square feet
	  d. Notes (operations manager uses this to capture distinguishing information)
	  e. Related documents (for example, a reference to a page in a plan or a blueprint)

Use Case A.6   *Establish Units (continues)*

Exceptions:	None
Postconditions:	The set of units is available to the system for reporting and leases.
Business Rules:	A unit may not be deleted if it has an active tenant.
Technical Requirements:	None
Notes:	Many of our buildings have intricate maps drawn of the unit layout. A nice-to-have requirement is the ability to store these diagrams and to associate them with the unit record. This is considered nice-to-have as the majority of the selling work is performed by commercial real estate agents.

Use Case A.6   *continued*

Use Case Name:	**Lease Property**
Description:	A property unit has been leased by a lessee. This use case allows the details of the lease to be recorded.
Actors:	Operations manager
Triggers:	A real estate management company informs the operations manager that a unit has been leased or that a change to a lease has been effected.
Preconditions:	The property and its units have been established in the system.

Basic Course of Events:	1. The operations manager navigates to the lease section—either directly, or by navigating to the property section first.
	 2. The system responds by displaying the set of units in the property together with their current lease status.
	 3. The operations manager may choose to alter an existing lease or to enter a new lease.
	 4. The system prompts the operations manager for the following:
	    a. Tenant details including identity, address, source of credit rating
	    b. Lease details including contract number and unit identity

Use Case A.7   *Lease Property (continues)*

Exceptions:	None
Postconditions:	The status of unit and tenant is available for reporting.
Business Rules:	A unit may not be leased to a new tenant without current leases being terminated.
Technical Requirements:	None

Use Case A.7   *continued*

Use Case Name:	**Import Data**
Description:	External partners manage some of the properties. Typically, the external partners are joint owners of a property with the company—they own part of the property and they are responsible for maintaining and leasing the entire property. On a schedule, they provide data and often money to the company as per their agreement. This use case takes the data an external partner provides and imports it into the system where it will be stored and available for reporting.
Actors:	• External partner • Operations manager
Triggers:	External partners provide data on a regular schedule as stipulated by a contract. Each reporting period they prepare data and submit it to the company, triggering this use case.
Preconditions:	An agreement is in place between the external partner and the company.
Basic Course of Events:	1. The operations manager receives a set of data or notification that a set of data is created from the external partner. 2. The operations manager locates the property referred to by the data. 3. The operations manager navigates to the import external partner data. 4. The system responds by requesting the location of the external data. 5. The operations manager provides the location.

Use Case A.8   *Import Data (continues)*

	6. The system validates that the data refers to the correct property.
	7. The system reads the following data for a property:
	  a. A series of cash amounts with corresponding dates
	  b. A series of capital payments with corresponding dates
	8. The system associates this information with the property.
	9. The system displays the imported data to the operations manager for approval.
	  a. The operations manager examines the data and either approves it or cancels the operation.
	  b. If the data is approved, the system stores the data.

Exceptions:	5. If the system is unable to locate or access the data, the system alerts the operations manager and waits for an operations manager to provide an alternative location or to cancel the operation. 6. If the data does not refer to the expected property, the system alerts the operations manager and the use case terminates.
Postconditions:	None
Business Rules:	None
Technical Requirements:	Only one method of data transfer will be supported. This is to reduce system complexity and staff-training issues. A stakeholder stated that the external partners have very little technology and business automation, and suggested that a spreadsheet format would be a suitable mechanism.

Use Case A.8   *continued*

Use Case Name:	**Establish Cash Flow Schedule**
Description:	When a tenant leases a property unit, we predict that he or she will make a series of timely rent payments. The company uses this data to predict the return on a property.
Actors:	Operations manager
Triggers:	• A property unit is leased. • A change to a property unit lease occurs (for example, the rent is increased).

Use Case A.9   *Establish Cash Flow Schedule (continues)*

Preconditions:	• A property is leased to a tenant. • A property lease terminates or attributes of the lease involving time or money change. • Invoked by the lease property use case.
Basic Course of Events:	1. The operations manager locates the property/unit. 2. The operations manager navigates to the cash flow functional area. 3. The system displays the existing cash flow schedule for the tenant, if one exists. This is made up of a sequence of dates, each with a dollar cash flow. 4. The operations manager adds, modifies, and deletes cash flows until satisfied that the series properly represents the terms of the lease.
Exceptions:	4. The system checks each entry against the cash flow business rules and if the data fails validation, the system alters the actor and does not accept the changes.
Postconditions:	None
Business Rules:	• A cash flow is a dollar amount paired with a date and optionally a memo field. • The dollar amount must be numeric. • The data cannot predate the lease, nor can it be dated after the lease is scheduled to end.
Technical Requirements:	From an interface design perspective, we need to find a way to decrease the amount of time taken to enter and review cash flow sequences. For example, provide an interface mechanism to repeat a cash flow for a set period (monthly) until a given date. We do not want to lose this data; provide the ability to cancel changes and to undo changes.
Notes:	There are no requirements for foreign currency.

Use Case A.9   *continued*

Use Case Name:	**Record Transactions**
Description:	Enter actual lease/rent payments on a regular basis.
Actors:	Operations manager
Triggers:	Regularly scheduled, at month end
Preconditions:	At least one property unit has been leased.

Basic Course of Events:	1. The operations manager locates the property/unit.
	2. The operations manager navigates to the transaction area.
	3. The operations manager enters in actual reconciled transactions, each with the following data:
	   a. Transaction date
	   b. Transaction type
	   c. Transaction amount
	   d. Optional memo field

Exceptions:	
Postconditions:	
Business Rules:	
Technical Requirements:	There are no current requirements for importing this data from either the book of record (account system) or from bank account data. This is a possibility for future projects, and the flexibility to add an automated interface would be appreciated.

Use Case A.10   *Record Transactions*

Use Case Name:	**Dispose of Property**
Description:	When a property is sold, or if the company has leased the property and subleased the units and the lease terminated, or if for other reasons the property will not be managed by the company at some date, it is necessary to record this.
Actors:	Operations manager
Triggers:	A property will cease to be managed by the company.
Preconditions:	The property was managed by the company.

Use Case A.11   *Dispose of Property (continues)*

Basic Course of Events:	1. The operations manager locates the property in the system. 2. The operations manager enters a date for the disposal of the property. 3. Optionally, the operations manager enters a transaction to cover any monetary change that results from the disposal. 4. The system deallocates all units that were leased and records the lease termination date. 5. The system removes all cash flows for the property from the termination date forward.
Exceptions:	
Postconditions:	
Business Rules:	
Technical Requirements:	

Use Case A.11 *continued*

Use Case Name:	**Establish Capital Schedule**
Description:	When the company acquires a property a capital schedule should be created to predict the payments the company will make to acquire, keep, and maintain the property. The company uses this data to predict the return on a property.
Actors:	Operations manager
Triggers:	• A property is acquired for management by the company through either outright purchase or via a lease. • Enter Property Details use case.
Preconditions:	None
Basic Course of Events:	1. The operations manager navigated to the capital schedule functional area. 2. The system displays the existing capital schedule for the tenant if one exists. This is made up of a sequence of dates, each with a dollar value and optionally a memo field.

Use Case A.12 *Establish Capital Schedule (continues)*

	3. The operations manager adds, modifies, and deletes capital values until satisfied that the series is realistic. These include any payments on notes, property taxes, and so on. 4. The system adds additional capital values from a set of rules. These include anticipated depreciation.
Exceptions:	4. The system checks each entry against the cash flow business rules, and if the data fails validation, the system alters the actor and does not accept the changes.
Postconditions:	None
Business Rules:	• A schedule item is a dollar amount, a date, a type, and optionally a memo field. • The dollar amount must be numeric. • Depreciation is assumed to be 1/12 of the annual expected revenue.
Technical Requirements:	• From an interface design perspective, we need to find a way to decrease the amount of time taken to enter these sequences. For example, provide an interface mechanism to repeat an item for a set period (monthly) until a given date. • We do not want to lose this data; provide the ability to cancel changes and to undo changes.
Notes:	There are no requirements for foreign currency.

Use Case A.12 *continued*

Use Case Name:	**Report Top Ten Properties**
Description:	This report calculates the actual internal rate of return (IRR) on each property managed by the company and reports on the ten properties with the highest IRR.
Actors:	Property manager
Triggers:	Create Reports use case
Preconditions:	None

Use Case A.13 *Report Top Ten Properties (continues)*

Basic Course of Events:	1. The system prompts user to enter the report "as of" date.
	2. The system calculates the IRR of each property from inception to the "as of" date.
	3. The system creates a printed report that contains the following data:
	   a. Rank: 1–10, where 1 indicates the highest IRR
	   b. IRR: The internal rate of return for the property
	   c. Property inception date
	   d. Property MSA: The location of the property
	   e. Property manager
	   f. Total property revenue
	4. The system invokes the appropriate use case for the report.

Exceptions:	2. If more than one property has the same IRR, both properties are given the same rank.
Postconditions:	Report for a given "as of" date is created.
Business Rules:	
Technical Requirements:	

Use Case A.13 *continued*

Use Case Name:	**Report Properties per MSA**
Description:	This report displays the name and other attributes of each property grouped by MSA. The actor uses this to determine geographical exposure.
Actors:	Property manager
Triggers:	Create Reports use case
Preconditions:	None
Basic Course of Events:	1. The system prompts user to enter the report "as of" date. 2. The system gathers the following data and prepares a report grouped by MSA: a. Property MSA: The location of the property

Use Case A.14 *Report Properties per MSA (continues)*

	b. Property Name c. Property inception date d. At the grouping level (MSA) the number of properties in the MSA are displayed. e. At the total level the total number of properties are displayed.
Exceptions:	2. MSAs that contain no properties are not included on the report.
Postconditions:	Report for a given "as of" date is created.
Business Rules:	
Technical Requirements:	

Use Case A.14   *continued*

Use Case Name:	**Report Expected Rate of Return**
Description:	This report displays the IRR anticipated for a property. Actual cash flows are used where transaction data is available; otherwise the cash flow schedule is used. The IRR is calculated for the completed lifespan of the property.
Actors:	Property manager
Triggers:	Create Reports use case
Preconditions:	None

Basic Course of Events:	1. The system prompts user to enter the report "as of" date.
	2. The system prompts property manager to select the property from a list.
	3. The system calculates the IRR and the following data and prepares a report:
	  a. Property Name
	  b. Property inception date
	  c. IRR
	  d. Sum of capital expenditures
	  e. Sum of lease payments
	  f. Transaction data available from date to date.

Use Case A.15   *Report Expected Rate of Return (continues)*

Exceptions:	None
Postconditions:	Report for a given "as of" date is created.
Business Rules:	
Technical Requirements:	

Use Case A.15   *continued*

Use Case Name:	**Report Exposure**
Description:	This report displays all properties in a specific MSA. This report is used to locate properties, perhaps based on a customer request.
Actors:	Operations manager
Triggers:	Create Reports use case
Preconditions:	None

Basic Course of Events:	1. The system prompts the user to enter the report "as of" date.
	2. The system prompts operations manager to select an MSA from a list.
	3. The system collates the following data and prepares a report:
	  a. MSA Name
	  b. Property Name
	  c. Property inception date
	  d. Number of vacant units
	  e. Number of total units

Exceptions:	None
Postconditions:	Report for a given "as of" date is created.
Business Rules:	
Technical Requirements:	

Use Case A.16   *Report Exposure*

Use Case Name:	**Report Property Utilization**
Description:	This report displays all properties that have an occupancy rate of less than 100 percent.
Actors:	Operations manager
Triggers:	Create Reports use case
Preconditions:	None

Basic Course of Events:	1. The system prompts the user to enter the report "as of" date.
	 2. The system collates the following data and prepares a report:
	   a. MSA Name
	   b. Property Name
	   c. Property inception date
	   d. Number of vacant units
	   e. Number of total units

Exceptions:	None
Postconditions:	Report for a given "as of" date is created.
Business Rules:	
Technical Requirements:	

Use Case A.17   *Report Property Utilization*

Use Case Name:	**Report Open Units per MSA**
Description:	This report displays all properties that have an occupancy rate of less than 100 percent grouped by MSA.
Actors:	Operations manager
Triggers:	Create Reports use case
Preconditions:	None
Basic Course of Events:	1. The system prompts user to enter the report "as of" date.

Use Case A.18   *Report Open Units per MSA (continues)*

	2. The system collates the following data and prepares a report:
	  a. MSA Name
	  b. Property Name
	  c. Property inception date
	  d. Number of vacant units
	  e. Number of total units
	3. The system groups the report by MSA and orders in the decreasing ratio of vacant to total units.

Exceptions:	None
Postconditions:	Report for a given "as of" date is created
Business Rules:	
Technical Requirements:	

Use Case A.18   *continued*

Use Case Name:	**Report Leases Expiring**
Description:	This report displays all properties that have leases due to expire within three months of the "as of" date.
Actors:	Operations manager
Triggers:	Create Reports use case
Preconditions:	None

Basic Course of Events:	1. The system prompts user to enter the report "as of" date.
	2. The system collates the following data and prepares a report:
	  a. Property Name
	  b. Lease Name
	  c. Lease expiration date
	  d. Current number of vacant units
	  e. Number of total units
	  f. Property MSA
	3. The system groups the report by lease expiration month and orders in the decreasing ratio of vacant to total units.

Use Case A.19   *Report Leases Expiring (continues)*

Exceptions:	None
Postconditions:	Report for a given "as of" date is created.
Business Rules:	
Technical Requirements:	

Use Case A.19   *continued*

Use Case Name:	**Import Index Information**
Description:	Rates of return on an investment are compared with returns on similar investments during the same period. Companies track the rates of return for leasing and sell this data. Property managers include indexes in performance reports to provide a comparison baseline.
Actors:	Operations manager
Triggers:	New index data becomes available.
Preconditions:	None
Basic Course of Events:	1. Navigate to the index data import area. 2. Select the data source from the system-displayed list. 3. Enter the "as of" date of the index data. 4. The system prompts actor to identify the location and name of the index data file. 5. The actor enters the location and name of the file. 6. The system attempts to open the file. 7. The system reads the data and verifies that the format and data types meet expectations. 8. The system stores the index data.
Exceptions:	6. If the system cannot find or open the file, alert the actor and return to step 4. 7. If the data or the file format do not meet expectations, alert the actor that the file may be corrupted and exit this use case.
Postconditions:	If the system was able to read and import the data file, index data for the "as of" date is available for reporting.

Use Case A.20   *Import Index Information (continues)*

Business Rules:	
Technical Requirements:	The technical requirements will vary by index data provider. Currently, only one type of index is being used—this is expected to change. Note that competing vendors have different file formats, although all of them use a flat file. A nice-to-have requirement is to simplify the ability to add additional types of indexes to the system after the initial implementation. The current file format used is a comma-separated file with the following fields

#	Field	Descr	Notes
1	Start Date	Begin period date	MMDDCCYY
2	End Date	End period date	MMDDCCYY
3	MSA	Metropolitan statistical area	MSA code
4	Return	IRR	Percentage with three decimal places

Use Case A.20 *continued*

Use Case Name:	**Set Up MSA**
Description:	MSA describes a geographical area at a higher level than zip code (it is similar to identifying the major city catchment area). This data is used to classify where properties are located.
Actors:	Operations manager
Triggers:	MSA data becomes available or is altered.
Preconditions:	None
Basic Course of Events:	1. Navigate to the MSA setup area. 2. The system responds by displaying the list of MSAs currently stored by the system.

Use Case A.21 *Set Up MSA (continues)*

	3. In any order, operations manager
	a. Adds an MSA
	i. The operations manager enters the MSA name.
	ii. The system verifies that the MSA name is longer than three characters and that it does not contain illegal characters (not alphanumeric or containing a space or "-").
	iii. The system stores the new MSA.
	iv. The system makes the new MSA available to other users of the system.
	b. Edits an existing MSA
	i. The operations manager selects an existing MSA.
	ii. The operations manager enters the name.
	iii. The system checks that the name is unique. If an MSA already exists with that name, the system alerts the operations manager.
	iv. The system verifies that the MSA name is longer than three characters and that it does not contain illegal characters (not alphanumeric or containing a space or "-").
	v. The system stores the new MSA.
	vi. The system makes the new MSA available to other users of the system.
	c. Deletes an MSA
	i. The operations manager selects an existing MSA.
	ii. The system checks that there are no properties or tenants currently "using" the MSA, and if there are none, the system removes the MSA from the store.
Exceptions:	cii. The system displays the set of properties and tenants that use the MSA. The operations manager is alerted that the MSA cannot be removed until no property or tenant is attached.
Postconditions:	Legal MSAs are added or altered in the system, and used MSAs may be removed.
Business Rules:	MSAs cannot be removed if they are referred to by a property or tenant.
Technical Requirements:	None

Use Case A.21   *continued*

Use Case Name:	**Set Up Users**
Description:	Users are identities actors interact with and use while interacting with the system. Each is associated with a real person and with the role the person has with the company.
Actors:	Operations manager
Triggers:	• A new employee is hired by the company. • A employee's role within the company changes. • An employee leaves the company. • An employee can no longer access the system due to expired or lost identity.
Preconditions:	None

Basic Course of Events:	1. Navigate to the administration, user area.
	2. The operations manager performs any of the following:
	  a. Add a user
	    i. The system prompts the operations manager for username, first and last names, user name and password, and role (selected from a list).
	    ii. The operations manager enters the required information.
	    iii. The system checks that first and last name fields are not empty and prompts the operations manager for more information if necessary.
	    iv. The system checks that the user name and password conform to the standard and, if necessary, prompts for a stronger user name and password combination.
	    v. The system stores the user data and grants the user rights within the system.
	  b. Reset a user
	    i. The system displays the set of users.
	    ii. The operations manager selects a user to reset.
	    iii. The system resets the password to the original and displays the original to the operations manager (who is expected to communicate the password to the user).
	    iv. The system flags the user account as reset.

Use Case A.22   *Set Up Users (continues)*

	c. Remove a user
	   i. The system displays the set of users.
	   ii. The operations manager selects a user to delete.
	   iii. The system marks the user as deleted and permits no further access.
	d. Edit a user
	   i. The system displays the set of users.
	   ii. The operations manager selects a user to edit.
	   iii. The system displays the first and last name and the username.
	   iv. The operations manager edits the information and submits it.
	   v. The system checks that the first and last name fields are not empty and prompts the operations manager for more information, if necessary.
	   vi. The system stores the user information.

Exceptions:	
Postconditions:	
Business Rules:	• Reset accounts must have their passwords changed to a new password the next time it is accessed, or the account will be locked. • Accounts that are not accessed within 24 hours of being reset are locked again.
Technical Requirements:	The security discussion revealed that the system should have reasonably strong security—the property managers want to protect sensitive information. A technical requirement that came from this is that all system access needs to be logged

Use Case A.22 *continued*

A.4 Refining the Requirements

This section describes our activities after the initial work of filling out the use cases is completed. We have questions listed in our notes that we will resolve, together with some opportunities for tightening the requirements, trimming scope, and making the system a more coherent whole. The next subsections focus on the changes we make to the filled use case, and where appropriate, explain our thinking behind these changes.

A.4.1 Investment Returns Calculation

After completing this round of detail-gathering, our fundamental view that this system is divided into data collection and reporting remains fundamentally unchanged. We realize that one important part of reporting—returns—can benefit from being examined more closely. Briefly, returns data will describe how an investment performed.

Property managers use calculation to determine how well their investments performed, and to predict how changes to an investment (for example, increasing the lease price) could alter that performance. The IRR is a standard business calculation for this task. We define IRR as the interest rate that makes net present value of all cash flow equal zero.[1] In the past, the operations manager has calculated the IRR in a spreadsheet. This is a time-consuming and error-prone process, as the IRR calculation uses the entire set of cash flows over the life of the investment. For leasing a building, this includes the initial principal used to acquire the property and every anticipated lease payment. For these reasons, adding the ability to perform this calculation to our system makes sense. We consider making a small use case just for this calculation, and plan to "attach" it to the reporting requirements use cases that include this data.

Use Case A.23 is the first draft of this use case.

Use Case Name:	Calculate Internal Rate of Return (IRR)
Description:	IRR is a standard business calculation based on regularly occurring cash flows that results in a description of the return (%) on an investment. This calculation will be used by a number of reports.
Actors:	Reporting use case
Triggers:	A report that includes IRR is being generated.
Preconditions:	For this calculation to complete, a set of cash flows, including at least one negative cash flow, must be available.

Basic Course of Events:	1. The system checks that the required data is available.
	  a. The first cash flow in the sequence must be negative.
	  b. The cash flows must form a regular sequence (that is, monthly, weekly, yearly, or similar).

Use Case A.23 *Calculate Internal Rate of Return (IRR) (continues)*

---

1. http://www.investopedia.com/terms/i/irr.asp

	c. Note that there will be other restrictions on the data that will only become apparent when the equation is analyzed by a programmer/designer to prevent errors such as "divide by zero." 2. The system implements the formula and returns the result.
Exceptions:	2. If the system is unable to complete the calculation, it returns the value ERROR.
Postconditions:	The system either rejected the cash flows, returned an error, or returned the IRR.
Business Rules:	Cash flows from the company to other parties are considered negative; cash flows from external parties to the company, for example, lease payments, are considered positive.
Technical Requirements:	Speed-users will not be prepared to wait more than 2 minutes for a report to be produced.

Use Case A.23   *continued*

So, with our draft of this calculating use case in hand, we consider how it will fit with our understanding of the requirements. Note that at this point we have avoided making any design decision on how the system will calculate the equation; we have also only defined the equation very loosely, and have instead told the business analysts and programmers that will inherit this set of requirements that they have some research to do to understand the equation, the various refinements to it, and any algorithms or heuristics developed by others to actually perform this calculation.

We attach this use case to our existing document for the reports.

Here we are stating that the Top Ten Properties and Expected Rate of Return reports will use the Calculate Internal Rate of Return use case. We also know that there are several other reports that will need to use this use case also.

Next we consider the requirement implicit in our use case—that the returns data must be calculated each time it is used. Our motivation here is to understand if this indeed needs to be a requirement, or if this data could be stored by the system just like the "static" data about tenants.

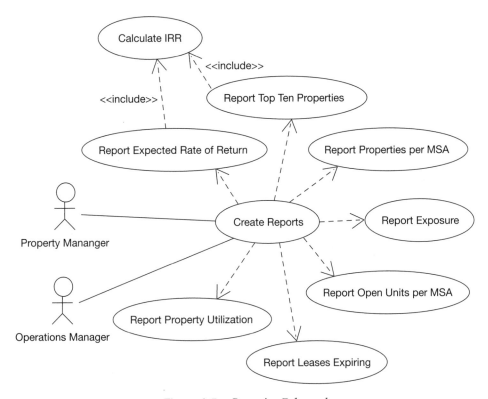

Figure A.5   *Reporting Enhanced*

A.4.2 Tightening Requirements

If the underlying data changes (for example, if we discover that the operations manager entered an incorrect lease payment last year), the calculation must be redone. This observation leads us to define a problem—the calculation results cannot be safely stored. This impacts the reporting requirements; IRR data may have to be treated differently than the other data. This affects the technical requirements for reports that include IRR since general reporting tools (Actuate and Crystal Reports to name two) are easiest to use when pulling data, via SQL, from a database system.

We discussed, with a subject matter expert, the likelihood of how and when data changes and determined that whenever data (capitalization and cash flow) change, we will require that the IRR be recalculated. We do not want to make a design decision at this point—we are only gathering requirements—so we alter the use case to capture our understanding of the business users' needs, and to highlight this area to ensure that people will notice it further down the lifecycle. Here is the altered form of the use case.

Use Case Name:	**Calculate Internal Rate of Return (IRR)**
Description:	IRR is a standard business calculation based on regularly occurring cash flows that results in a description of the return (%) on an investment. This calculation will be used by a number of reports.
Actors:	Reporting use case
Triggers:	• A report that includes IRR is being generated for one or more properties. • Cash flow data for a property changed, and the IRR for that property will be included on a report. • Capitalization data for a property changed, and the IRR of that property will be included on a report.
Preconditions:	For this calculation to complete, a set of cash flows, including at least one negative cash flow, must be available.

Basic Course of Events:	1. The system checks that the required data is available.
	   a. The first cash flow in the sequence must be negative.
	   b. The cash flows must form a regular sequence (that is, monthly, weekly, yearly, or similar).
	   c. Note that there will be other restrictions on the data that will only become apparent when the equation is analyzed by a programmer/designer to prevent errors such as divide by zero.
	2. The system implements the formula and returns the result.

Exceptions:	2. If the system is unable to complete the calculation, it returns the value ERROR.
Postconditions:	The system either rejected the cash flows, returned an error, or returned the IRR.
Business Rules:	Cash flows from the company to other parties are considered negative; cash flows from external parties to the company, for example, lease payments, are considered positive.
Technical Requirements:	Speed-users will not be prepared to wait more than 2 minutes for a report to be produced.

Use Case A.24 *Calculate Internal Rate of Return (IRR)*

There are many technical options available to tackle this problem. These will be explored by the team as a design task, and the decisions made can be made primarily on cost, since the baseline requirement has been calculated.

After reviewing the current set of requirements with the stakeholders, we dig further into some of them—for example, the technical requirement for MSA—and we find that this database is available in comma-separated format as a subscription that is updated regularly. Since the returns indexes available use MSA, it is important to the managers that MSA is kept current; therefore a new requirement appears to be the ability to automate the import of the MSA data. Further discussion reveals that it is not anticipated that the existing MSA for a property will change; therefore we do not need sophisticated automation to deal with this possibility.

Use Case Name:	**Import MSA Data**
Description:	MSA data defines broad location areas in the United States; they are less specific than cities and are closer to saying the "Greater NY area." MSA is important to us as organizations predict how profitable real estate investments should be based on their location. Our system tracks MSA data for each property, and we need to keep that information up-to-date, corresponding to its release by the United States Postal Service.
Actors:	Operations manager
Triggers:	A new data set is received.
Preconditions:	None
Basic Course of Events:	1. The operations manager loads the media containing the csv file. 2. The operations manager navigates to the maintenance area and selects Load MSA from the system-supplied options. 3. The system prompts the operations manager for the location and name of the csv file. 4. The system reads the file and verifies that its contents are as expected. 5. The system creates a backup of the existing MSA data set.

Use Case A.25   *Import MSA Data (continues)*

	6. The system copies the data from the csv file to its datastore. 7. The system verifies that all MSAs in use by the systems set of properties refer to a valid MSA.
Exceptions:	7. If a property's MSA is not available in the new data set, the system alters the actor and identifies the affected property(ies) and MSA. The operations manager will research the problem and, if necessary, enter a new MSA for the affected property.
Postconditions:	• The system contains an updated set of MSA data. • All existing properties in the system refer to a valid MSA.
Business Rules:	
Technical Requirements:	

Use Case A.25 *continued*

At this point, the requirements are sufficiently close to being available for realization that it is safe to begin work in the other system-development activities.

B

Integrated Systems

B.1 Overview

This example demonstrates the relationship between business and technical requirements. We selected this example because it includes technical requirements that are not purely concerned with the usual suspects of load, stress, and scalability. We approach this example as change to an existing use case without showing the steps that led to the development of the requirements up to this point.

Our starting point is the realization that our system has a serious flaw—we missed an important requirement—and development is already under way.

B.2 Background

This system, being built for a government agency, consists of a number of off-the-shelf components (workflow, imaging, and accounting systems) integrated with proprietary business software. Its overall function is to enroll applicants into a retirement system. The business is triggered when an enrollment form is received. The form is scanned electronically using an enterprise scale imaging system and the original is sent to document storage. The type of form received indicates the business process the sender requested, and the system creates an instance of this process in the workflow system. The next available operator will be assigned this work and will access the document image from the integrated system if the client has an active account that is made available.

Figure B.1   *Enroll Retirement System Member*

This short description indicates that several systems integrate to handle this business—imaging, workflow, accounts, and the propriety business systems. Here is the original use case describing the requirements for one activity—enrolling users. We will work with a high-level use case, as the issue we will explore does not lie in the details.

Use Case Name:	**Enroll Member**
Description:	The agency received an application from a person who wanted to join the retirement system. Determine his eligibility and, if necessary, record the enrollment details and create the account.
Actors:	Enrollment specialist
Triggers:	A person submitted an application to join the retirement system.
Preconditions:	The Create Process from the Received Mail use case is completed.

Basic Course of Events:	1. The system notifies the actor that a membership application was received.
	2. The actor accepts the work assignment.
	3. The system displays the received application.
	4. The actor examines the application to determine eligibility.
	5. The system prompts the actor for eligibility information including
	   a. Agency of employment
	   b. Hours per month
	   c. Employment date

Use Case B.1   *Enroll Member (continues)*

	6. The system determines eligibility.
	7. The system prompts the actor to enter data for account creation, including
	   a. Name
	   b. Address
	   c. Social Security Number
	8. The system creates a new account for the member.
	   a. New retirement account
	   b. Electronic document account
	9. The system moves the enrollment form from the processing queue to the members account.
	10. The system marks the workflow instance as complete.
	11. The system updates the actor's work record to indicate the start and end time of this process.

Exceptions:	6. If the prospective member is found ineligible, the system creates a rejection notice to be printed and mailed (see Send Form Letter use case).
Postconditions:	• The enrollment form is removed from the "received" queue. • The enroll member business process instance is marked as completed.
Business Rules:	Refer to enrollment business rules (for brevity these are not listed here).
Technical Requirements:	None

Use Case B.1 *continued*

B.3 Problem Description

The above use case went through extensive analysis and discussion with the team and stakeholders. It is core to the philosophy behind the system, and was new to the client and the team. Mainframe systems were simpler, less elaborate, and more focused on storing bare-bones data and implementing rules. It was not until the initial design iteration and the first build completed that a large issue came to light: Each integrated system is independent, and there was no notion of a transaction across the breadth of systems.

A new enrollment process first stored the document image, then created a shell account with the minimum possible data, then created a "new account setup" workflow event. If, for example, the workflow event creation failed, there were serious consequences:

The imaging folder contained an orphaned image, the business system contained an account that contained insufficient data for business, and the enrollee would not have an account created and would never receive an acknowledgment. In short, the system would fail. The problem statement is this: The initial requirements did not specify how exceptions should be handled across the integrated systems.

B.4 Solution Analysis

The root of the problem is that a set of requirements and business rules were missed during analysis.

We return to the Filled Level use case and add the following requirement to the exceptions: "The account setup, workflow task, and captured images are essential to this business process; if any of these fail, delete their partners and repeat this use case until successful."

Here is the use case revised.

Use Case Name:	**Enroll Member**
Description:	The agency received an application from a person who wanted to join the retirement system. Determine eligibility and, if necessary, record the enrollment details and create the account.
Actors:	Enrollment specialist
Triggers:	A person submitted an application to join the retirement system.
Preconditions:	The Create Process from the Received Mail use case was completed.
Basic Course of Events:	1. The system notifies the actor that a membership application was received. 2. The actor accepts the work assignment. 3. The system displays the received application. 4. The actor examines the application to determine eligibility. 5. The system prompts actor for eligibility information include a. Agency of employment b. Hours per month c. Employment date

Use Case B.2 *Enroll Member (continues)*

	6. The system determines eligibility.
	7. The system prompts the actor to enter data for account creation, including
	a. Name
	b. Address
	c. Social Security Number
	8. The system creates a new account for the member
	a. New retirement account
	b. Electronic document account
	9. The system moves the enrollment form from the processing queue to the members account.
	10. The system marks the workflow instance as complete.
	11. The system updates the actor's work record to indicate the start and end time of this process.
Exceptions:	6. If the prospective member is found ineligible, the system creates a rejection notice to be printed and mailed (see the Send Form Letter use case).
	7. *If any step in the account creation process fails, roll back all of the other steps.*
Postconditions:	• The enrollment form is removed from the "received" queue.
	• The enroll member business process instance is marked as completed.
Business Rules:	• Refer to enrollment business rules (for brevity these are not listed here)
	• An account is made up of
	– *A business account (in the custom system)*
	– *An account in the imaging/document management system*
	• *Both are required for a valid account.*
Technical Requirements:	None

Use Case B.2   *continued*

Note that we do not specify how any of the rollbacks will be accomplished. We only want to document what needs to be done.

C

Instant Messaging Encryption

C.1 Overview

During the last two years, we have been using instant messaging clients for more and more communication. Typically, we use it for business, as it is a free way to have a four-way discussion as opposed to costly conference calling. There is a big disadvantage though—our business is traversing the Internet in plain-text form. One answer would be to encrypt the message stream so that only bona fide partners may read our smiley-laden communication. We are aware that several companies are selling solutions to this problem, and we have decided to write our requirements as a precursor to the acquisition process. This allows us to focus on our needs before we are influenced by the various solutions.

C.2 The Use Cases

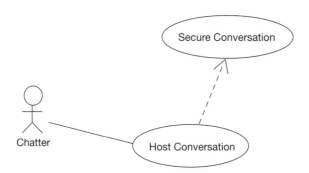

Figure C.1   *Encrypt Conversation*

Use Case Name:	**Host Conversation**
Description:	This corresponds to the functionality provided by a typical instant messaging client. The IM Client is used to select with whom to converse, and text messages are passed to all connected clients.
Actors:	Chatter
Preconditions:	• Instant messaging requires an account to be set up. • To select conversation partners, their identities must be entered into the system. • An internet connection must be established.
Basic Course of Events:	1. Chatter initiates a conversation. 2. The system displays a set of identities available for conversation. 3. Select the parties for the conversation. 4. Initiate the conversation by typing a message. 5. The system displays the typed message to all selected identities. 6. When a user is typing, and before she submits the text to the party, the system broadcasts to all other conversation parties that the user is typing. This helps prevent people from interrupting a conversation flow.

Use Case C.1   *Host Conversation (continues)*

	7. When a user leaves the conversation, the system displays a message to the other parties of the conversation stating who left. This only occurs if there are more than two parties to the conversation.
Exceptions:	1. If another user initiates the conversation, the system displays the message to the intended recipient. All Steps: If a user's network connection is disrupted, it has the same effect as if the user voluntarily left the conversation.
Postconditions:	When the conversation is complete, the system removes all state information.

Use Case C.1   *continued*

After taking the five minutes to clarify the essential functions of the instant messaging software to ourselves, we begin our preliminary analysis of the functionality we require from the encryption solution.

Use Case Name:	**Secure Conversation**
Description:	Encrypt the transfer of information between instant messaging clients to prevent the conversation from being vulnerable on a public network.
Actors:	Host Conversation use case
Preconditions:	• An instant message application is being used to connect one or more chatters in a common conversation. • The parties to the conversation also have the ability to execute this use case (i.e., they have the encryption software).
Basic Course of Events:	1. The system detects that the instant messaging client is attempting to establish a conversation with one or more other parties (the invocation of Host Conversation use case).

Use Case C.2   *Secure Conversation (continues)*

	2. The system determines if each party is able to support encryption. • If any of the parties are unable to support encryption, the system displays a message to all parties stating that the session will not be secure. • Otherwise, the system encrypts all messages sent. 3. When the instant messaging client receives a message, the system intercepts the message, decrypts the message, and passes it to the instant message use case.
Exceptions:	None
Postconditions:	The system maintains a log of the entire conversation and the identities of the participants.

Use Case C.2 *continued*

At this point we have a better idea of what we are really looking for, and how we want to interact with it. We also notice that we have strayed from the point of encryption just slightly with the addition of the postcondition regarding the logging. This came about when we discussed what the state of the system should be when we complete the use case. First, we did not want to have any additional steps to take—the convenience of instant messaging is important to us, and increasing the number of steps needed would not be a good thing! After determining that we wanted simplicity, we immediately added a requirement for logging. We all realized that the log, and the functionality behind it, is probably best represented by a separate use case, but that is not practical at this point in our analysis. Our compromise—to add it as a postcondition and think further about it later—beats losing that thought forever.

Armed with this set of sketched-out requirements, we are confident in evaluating other people's solutions. Note that we would not consider these to be sufficient requirements to begin elaborating a project in which we built this software, however.

D

Order a Product from a Catalog

Anoto created a technology involving special paper and pens that has very interesting applications. It gives paper the flexibility and capabilities of electronic systems and closes the gap between the ease of use of paper and the processing capabilities of computers. Briefly, the technology works like this: Paper has a near-invisible pattern printed on it that identifies the "application" the paper is for, and uniquely addresses each area of the paper sheet. The pen contains a tiny video camera that reads the pattern on the paper, allowing it to record what is written, and where. Many applications, ranging from medical charts to day planners, have been proposed for this technology.

For this example, we write a high-level set of use cases to define an application that uses the Anoto system. This will demonstrate use cases that have system actors, and how use cases are a tool for exploring a new system. The application is an enhancement to a catalog ordering system. The premise is to employ the Anoto technology to make it simple for existing customers to order from a catalog. To achieve this, we plan to print the product catalog on Anoto patterned paper and mail our catalog to our existing customers. Of course, these customers will have to own an Anoto capable pen, but since these have been released by companies such as Logitech and Sony-Erricson, we feel justified in the risk of planning our marketing campaign (which includes specifying the software) and determining the feasibility of our idea before the technology is widely adapted.

Each page in the catalog will be printed on top of the unique pattern that we will license from Anoto. Except for this near-invisible pattern, the catalog will look exactly like our existing catalog—each page shows pictures, specifications, and prices for a variety of merchandise. Until now, we have given consumers three ways to purchase our goods: mail, telephone, and Web. Often, customers will find articles in a paper catalog and then visit our Web site to order them. Since much of our business is impulsive ordering by repeat customers, we feel that by simplifying the steps a customer would take to complete a purchase after he has seen something interesting in the catalog, we can increase our sales. The addition of the Anoto pen will give the customer the ability to buy a product by marking the catalog entry for the item. Each product will have a "Buy Now" box printed near the product's price. The shopper only has to tick this box with an Anoto pen, and he will have the product delivered to his home.

We write up our initial understanding of the requirements as a use case description.

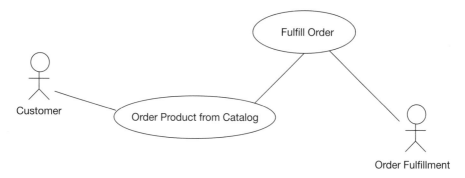

Figure D.1   *Order Product from Catalog*

Use Case Name:	**Order Product from Catalog**
Description:	A customer orders a product from our catalog by making a tick mark in the "Buy Now" box next to a catalog item.
Actors:	• *Customer*—An existing consumer to whom we ship our catalog, and who has an Anoto-enabled catalog • *Order Fulfillment*—A system that processes and ships inventory
Preconditions:	• The customer has requested the Anoto-enabled version of our catalog. • The customer has an Anoto-enabled pen.
Triggers:	The customer has found an item that he wants to purchase from our catalog.

Use Case D.1   *Order Product from Catalog (continues)*

Basic Course of Events:	1. The customer checks the "Buy Now" box in the catalog. 2. The order fulfillment system receives the product, quantity, and customer identity.
Exceptions:	None
Postconditions:	• The Fulfill Order use case is invoked. • The customer has placed a product order.

Use Case D.1 *continued*

Use Case Name:	**Fulfill Order**
Description:	A customer placed an order via the "Order Item from Catalog" use case; the system identifies the product and the customer account and prepares the order for delivery and invoicing.
Actors:	• Order Product from Catalog use case • *Order Fulfillment*—an existing system used for telephone and Web sales
Triggers:	A customer used an Anoto pen to order a product from the catalog.
Preconditions:	None
Basic Course of Events:	1. Identify the item for purchase by referencing the data provided by the Order Product from the Catalog user case. 2. Check that there is inventory of the item available. 3. Look up the customer's record by referencing the identity provided by the Pen. 4. Reduce the inventory to reflect the order. 5. Invoke the Deliver Order use case. This will debit the customer's credit card and ship the product.
Exceptions:	None
Postconditions:	The order is marked as suspended or fulfilled.

Use Case D.2 *Fulfill Order*

Our next step is to add detail to these use cases and to add an additional actor—a system actor that we call Pen. This use case represents the system and processing present in an Anoto

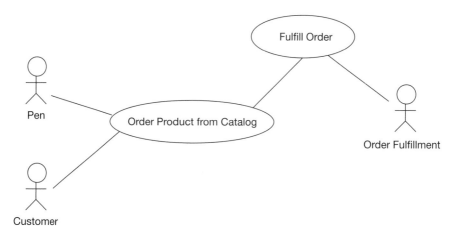

Figure D.2   *Order Product from Catalog—Enhanced*

pen used by a customer, and the overall connectivity used by the Pen to access servers and the Internet, including the Anoto service, which identifies the application from the paper and routes information from the pen to the registered application owner. Note that we do not have to open the "black box" of Anoto; we only concern ourselves with the details necessary for us to be consumers of this technology. With that in mind, we expand our use cases to get a better idea of the feasibility of our idea.

Use Case Name:	**Order Product from Catalog**
Description:	A customer orders a product from our catalog by making a tick mark in the "Buy Now" box next to a catalog item.
Actors:	• *Customer*—An existing consumer to whom we ship our catalog, and who has requested the Anoto-enabled catalog • *Order Fulfillment*—Our company's system that processes and ships inventory
Preconditions:	• The customer has requested the Anoto-enabled version of our catalog. • The customer has an Anoto-enabled pen.
Triggers:	The customer has found an item that he wants to purchase from our catalog.

Use Case D.3   *Order Product from Catalog (continues)*

Basic Course of Events:	1. The customer checks the "Buy now" box in the catalog.
	2. The Pen identifies the paper application—in this case our catalog—identifies the location on the page, and identifies that the "Buy Now" box has been checked.
	3. The Pen connects with the Anoto servers and passes the application identified.
	4. Anoto responds with an Internet address for our catalog application.
	5. The Pen sends the customer ID and the page location to our order fulfillment center.
Exceptions:	2. and 3. If the Pen is unable to make a connection, the Pen displays a status of "Error." Note that this is specific to the Pen's implementation and could be an audible or visible alert.
Postconditions:	• The Fulfill Order use case is invoked. • The customer has placed a product order.

Use Case D.3 *continued*

Use Case Name:	**Fulfill Order**
Description:	A customer placed an order via the "Order Item from Catalog" use case. The system identifies the product and the customer account and prepares the order for delivery and invoicing.
Actors:	• Order Product from Catalog use case • *Order Fulfillment*—An existing system used for telephone and Web sales
Triggers:	An Anoto pen transmitted an order to our servers.
Preconditions:	The Pen was able to identify the customer, the catalog, and the item being purchased for this use case to have been invoked.

Basic Course of Events:	1. Identify the catalog and version.
	2. If the catalog is out of date
	    a. Check that the item is still in inventory.
	    b. Compare the price of the item.

Use Case D.4 *Fulfill Order (continues)*

	3. Identify the item for purchase by referencing the unique page area provided by the Pen information. 4. Check that there is inventory of the item available. 5. Look up the customer's record by referencing the identity provided by the Pen. 6. Determine if the customer is set up for Anoto pen transactions. 7. Reduce the inventory to reflect the order. 8. Invoke the Deliver Order use case; this will debit the customer's credit card and ship the product.
Exceptions:	2a. If the item is out of inventory, send e-mail to the user explaining that the item is out of stock. 2b. If the price of the item has changed, and if the price has increased by more than 8%, send e-mail to the user explaining the price change and requesting that the user confirm the order at the new price. 3. If the catalog item cannot be identified, send e-mail to the customer explaining that the order was mishandled and cannot be delivered or invoiced. 4. If there is no inventory available, flag the order for review by an order clerk. The order clerk is responsible for ordering additional inventory and communicating the delay or cancellation to the customer. 5. If the customer cannot be found, that is, he is not an existing customer, send e-mail to the Pen user that includes a link to the sign-up area. Store the current order as suspended. 6. If the customer is not set up for Anoto pen transactions, mark the order as suspended and send the customer an e-mail that allows the transaction to be completed.
Postconditions:	The order is marked as suspended or fulfilled.
Business Rules:	• Catalogs are out of date (stale) if the "cover" date is greater than 18 months old. • *Stale prices*—When a customer orders goods from an out-of-date catalog, we will honor the original price if the change is no more than 8%. Otherwise, the order is suspended pending the customer agreeing to the new price.

Use Case D.4 *continued*

Bibliography

Alexander, C. 1996. Keynote address presented at the 1996 OOPSLA Conference, San Jose, CA.

Bass, L., P. Clements, R. Kazman. 2003. *Software Architecture in Practice (Second Edition)*, Addison-Wesley.

Bennett, D. 1997. *Designing Hard Software*, Prentice Hall.

Boehm, B. 1982. *Software Engineering Economics*, Prentice Hall PTR.

Boehm, B. 1986. "A Spiral Model of Software Development and Enhancement," *ACM SIGSOFT Software Engineering Notes*, August.

Boer, F. P., 2002. *The Real Options Solution: Finding Total Value in a High-Risk World*, John Wiley & Sons.

Booch, G., I. Jacobson, and J. Rumbaugh. 1998. *The Unified Modeling Language User Guide*, Addison-Wesley.

Cantor, M. 1998. *Object-Oriented Project Management with UML*, John Wiley & Sons.

Constantine, L., and L. Lockwood. 1999. *Software for Use: A Practical Guide to Models and Methods of Usage Centered Design*, Addison-Wesley.

Cooper, A. 1995. *About Face: The Essentials of User Interface Design*, IDG Books Worldwide.

de Bono, E. 1994. *de Bono's Thinking Course, Revised Edition*, Checkmark Books.

Drucker, P. 1993. *The Practice of Management*, Harper Business.

Gottesdiener, E. 2002. *Requirements by Collaboration Workshops for Defining Needs*, Addison-Wesley.

Guillory, W. 2000. *The Living Organization: Spirituality in the Workplace*, Innovations International.

Haeckel, S. 1999. *Adaptive Enterprise: Creating and Leading Sense-and-Respond Organizations*, Harvard Business School Press.

Highsmith, J. 2000. *Adaptive Software Development: A Collaborative Approach to Managing Complex Systems*, Dorset House.

Hock, D. 2000. *Birth of the Chaordic Age*, Berrett-Koehler.

Jacobson, I., G. Booch, and J. Rumbaugh. 1999. *The Unified Software Development Process*, Addison-Wesley.

Jacobson, I., M. Christerson, P. Jonsson, and G. Overgaard. 1992. *Object-Oriented Software Engineering: A Use Case Driven Approach*, Addison-Wesley.

Jacobson, Ivar. 1996. "Use Cases Tutorial," OOPSLA Conference, San Jose, CA.

Jacobson, Ivar. 1995. *The Object Advantage: Business Process Reengineering with Object Technology*, Addison-Wesley.

Jensen, R. 2001 (Reprint Edition). *The Dream Society: How the Coming Shift from Information to Imagination Will Transform Your Business,* McGraw-Hill Trade.

Jones, C. 1996. *Applied Software Measurement: Assuring Productivity and Quality*, 2d ed., McGraw Hill.

Larman, C. 2002. *Applying UML and Patterns, Second Edition: An Introduction to Object-Oriented Analysis and Design*, Prentice Hall.

McConnell, S. 1996. *Rapid Development: Taming Wild Software Schedules*, Microsoft Press.

Peters, T. 1991. *Thriving on Chaos: Handbook for a Management Revolution*, HarperCollins.

Pirsig, R. 1974. *Zen and the Art of Motorcycle Maintenance: An Inquiry into Values*, William Morrow & Company.

Ross, R. 1997. *The Business Rule Book: Classifying, Defining and Modeling Rules, Version 4.0*, Business Rules Solutions, Inc.

Royce, W. 1998. *Software Project Management: A Unified Framework*, Addison-Wesley.

Rumbaugh, J., I. Jacobson, and G. Booch. 1999. *The Unified Modeling Language Reference Manual*, Addison-Wesley.

Schneider, G., and J. Winters. 2001. *Applying Use Cases, Second Edition: A Practical Guide*, Addison-Wesley.

Sommerville, I., and P. Sawyer. 1997. *Requirements Engineering: A Good Practice Guide*, John Wiley & Sons.

Suh, N.P. 1990. *The Principles of Design*, Oxford University Press.

Waldrop, M. M. 1992. *Complexity: The Emerging Science at the Edge of Order and Chaos*, Touchstone Books.

Wheatley, M. 2001. *Leadership and the New Science, Second Edition: Discovering Order in a Chaotic World*, Berrett-Koehler.

Williams, T., and H. Li. 1992. *The Purdue Enterprise Reference Architecture*, Purdue University.

Index

Wouldn't it be great

if the world's leading technical publishers joined forces to deliver their best tech books in a common digital reference platform?

They have. Introducing
InformIT Online Books
powered by Safari.

Specific answers to specific questions.
ormIT Online Books' powerful search engine gives you evance-ranked results in a matter of seconds.

Immediate results.
ith InformIT Online Books, you can select the book u want and view the chapter or section you need mediately.

Cut, paste and annotate.
ste code to save time and eliminate typographical rors. Make notes on the material you find useful and oose whether or not to share them with your work oup.

Customized for your enterprise.
ustomize a library for you, your department or your entire ganization. You only pay for what you need.

Get your first 14 days FREE!
r a limited time, InformIT Online Books is offering members a 10 book subscription risk-free for 4 days. Visit **http://www.informit.com/online-** ooks for details.

informit.com/onlinebooks

Register
Your Book

at www.awprofessional.com/register

You may be eligible to receive:

- Advance notice of forthcoming editions of the book
- Related book recommendations
- Chapter excerpts and supplements of forthcoming titles
- Information about special contests and promotions throughout the year
- Notices and reminders about author appearances, tradeshows, and online chats with special guests

Contact us

If you are interested in writing a book or reviewing manuscripts prior to publication, please write to us at:

Editorial Department
Addison-Wesley Professional
75 Arlington Street, Suite 300
Boston, MA 02116 USA
Email: AWPro@aw.com

Visit us on the Web: http://www.awprofessional.com